Becoming Dads

A Mission to Restore Absent Fathers

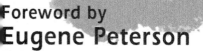

Foreword by
Eugene Peterson

Marvin Charles
with Jamie Bohnett

Becoming Dads: A Mission to Restore Absent Fathers
First Edition Trade Book, 2016
Copyright © 2016 by Marvin Charles

Scripture quotations are from the ESV® Bible (The Holy Bible, English Standard Version®), copyright © 2001 by Crossway, a publishing ministry of Good News Publishers. Used by permission. All rights reserved.

To Order:
Visit http://www.aboutdads.org

Also available at http://www.amazon.com

ISBN: 978-0-9976009-0-2

Published by: **ANYMAN** **PUBLISHING**

Editorial: Arlyn Lawrence, Inspira Literary Solutions, Gig Harbor, WA
Book Design: CarrotStick Marketing, Gig Harbor, WA
Printed in the USA by Ingram Spark, Nashville, TN

"Marvin Charles was born to lead. He has overcome a chaotic childhood, addictive behaviors, and many poor decisions to become a committed husband, a humble father, and a trailblazer in the national effort to restore the father/child relationship.

Marvin's on the ground leadership in greater Seattle has helped hundreds of fathers and children get reconnected. The success of his D.A.D.S. program and its outcomes distinguishes Marvin among many initiatives seeking to improve child well-being through responsible fatherhood. In his first book, *Becoming Dads: The Mission to Restore Absent Fathers*, he reveals his story, and the strategy and lessons he's learned about strengthening the father/child bond in the most difficult circumstances.

I heartily support and believe that Marvin and D.A.D.S. are leaving a legacy that will last. His book makes an important contribution to our understanding of the role fathers should play in their children's lives, and how to begin even if they are at 'ground zero.' Buy a copy; it's a quick read and you'll gain new insights in every chapter."

Ken R. Canfield, **Founder, National Center for Fathering**

"Marvin Charles' story will take you on a journey from hopelessness to victory, from ruin to restoration. His epic mission to restore absent fathers profoundly matters to anyone who cares about the deep impact of fatherlessness in this nation. Read *Becoming Dads*. No matter where you are, you'll find hope, find vision, find coaching, and find inspiration. In cities and suburbs, in rescue missions, prisons, or anywhere else, this story and mission must spread!"

Jeff Kemp, **Former NFL Quarterback, VP, FamilyLife, and author of** *Facing The Blitz*

"*Becoming Dads*, from its very first sentence, draws you in and holds you captive until its conclusion. It breaks your heart, and just when you think it can't get any worse—it does! But Marvin refuses to quit, not only in his efforts to break his own chain of pain, but his family's and his community's as well. This is an incredible story of hope, faith, and transformation! Someone should make a movie about Marvin and Jeanett's story of redemption."

Dr. Clarence Shuler, President/CEO, Building Lasting Relationships

"Our hearts hunger for true stories of redemption. Often, though, transformational, before-and-after stories sound too good to be true. Such is not the case for this account of Marvin and Jeanett Charles' life. It's painfully gritty, as it honestly portrays abandonment, rejection, and bad choices. Life is messy, and there is no neat, sweet, tied-up-with-a-pretty-bow kind of magical resolution. Rather, Marvin and Jeanett honestly portray the daily choices required to continue to walk "the straight life." They invite us to face with honesty, courage, and confidence the daily choice to seek God's redemption of the consequences of our past and the pains of the present, in anticipation of the joyous hope of the future.

There's yet another dimension to their story, one that speaks to us all. It's the story of our search for home, a place where we're safe, known, welcomed, and embraced. Through their own losses and restoration, Marvin and Jeanett have been used by God to help thousands of others come home—and I believe there's nothing our orphaned and homeless world needs more than to experience the welcoming embrace of our Heavenly Father, and the human embrace of our earthly ones."

Tim Dearborn, PhD., Director, Ogilvie Institute for Preaching, Fuller Theological Seminary

"I read this book in one sitting. Once I started reading, I couldn't put it down. The story of Marvin Charles' life is absolutely gripping and profoundly inspiring. He overcame huge personal challenges and is now helping other men do the same, with the help of God. I admire Marvin and his wife, Jeanett, more than any couple I've ever known."

John Hamer, Founder, Washington News Council

"*Becoming Dads* is beautifully written, thoughtfully presented, and impactful. I read the book in one day - literally couldn't put it down. It was eye-opening for me in many ways. I had not realized how the system rewards women who remain single, thus helping push fathers from their families. I also gained an understanding of just how seductive the "pimp and drug" outlaw style must be to a young man growing up in poverty. In Marvin's shoes, I wonder if I would have made the same choices. I applaud Marvin's courage in revealing the less heroic aspects of his life. Here lies is the brilliance of this book. Because of its searing honesty and intelligence, it carries the reader past judgment into compassion."

Sue Gilbert, Director, *Beyond Greenaway: The Legacy*

*To my lovely wife Jeanett, and my eight children:
Dontay, Nick, Marvin Jr. Jeffrey, Lyric, Devotion,
Marvette, and Jamie.*

*Marvette, you were the one
who really got this journey started.*

ACKNOWLEDGMENTS

I want to express my sincere appreciation for the many people from different sectors of my life that have contributed to my life and to this book. I will try my best to remember all of you, but if I don't, please blame it on my head and not my heart:

My birth parents, Doris and Willie, who gave me life, and the brothers, and sisters I was fortunate enough to have been reunited with before this life was over: Benoris, Audrey, Chris, and Hulett

Edward and Nora Charles, who had the courage to take two adopted children and raise them as their own

My sister, Marion Charles, my nieces Chessie and Lashawntae, and nephews Juion and Terence who saw the dark side and have also witnessed my life in the light

My brothers, Rick and Wesley Cotton, who gave me my first look at what I longed to have growing up—a family that would call me "son," and Wesley and Emma Cotton who actually called me their son: Marvin L. Charles-Cotton

My Uncle Larron, the best uncle a nephew could have

Mrs. Valerie Colursurdo, who, when I was eighteen, gave me a place to live and when I asked, "How will I ever pay you back for all that you've done for me?" simply said to pass it on

My dear friend Pastor Clarence Shuler, who prayed for me and impressed on me how much God loved me, and what amazing things He would entrust to me

All the people who contributed to make this book possible: Johnnie Gage, Levi Fisher, Ken & Dee Canfield, Art & Janet Kopicky, Allen & Margret Belton, Al & Doris Gillet, Paul & Susan Moulton, Matthew & Amy Welch, Sue Gilbert, Katie Tormey, Tyler & Kim Gorsline, Tyler & Jenn Jones, Michael Rogers, Stefano Gaudiano, Eddie Wang, Heidi Blake, Jim & Sara Caldwell, Debra Ronnholm Kevin Vitulli, Dennis Trittin, John Hamer, The Grove Family, Brenda Campbell, James Norris, Shane Morrison, Michelle, Brandon Jeremy Bohnett, and Richard Humphreys

David & Amy Pashane, Dave Ederer, Scott & Sara Campbell, Conrad & Judy Jacobsen and the Jacobsen Family, Randy & Heather Brothers, and Don Valencia

Jamie Bohnett, and his wife Colleen, who believed in what we wanted to do from the very start and that is why my little girl is named Jamie

Becoming DaDs

A Mission to Restore Absent Fathers

Foreword by
Eugene Peterson

Marvin Charles
with Jamie Bohnett

Marvin and Jeanett Charles

ABOUT THE AUTHORS

Min. Marvin L. Charles, Sr. is an ordained minister and the Founder and Executive Director of Divine Alternatives for Dads Services (D.A.D.S.), an organization dedicated to restoring absent fathers through supportive community, and helping navigate relational and legal barriers that separate them from their children. He is a frequent speaker across the U.S., speaking about empowering fathers and sharing his successes with other organizations hoping to follow his example. Marvin and his wife Jeanett are a living success story of family restoration and are the proud parents of eight children.

Jamie Bohnett has been an advocate for committed fatherhood in the greater Seattle area through his writing, facilitating of men's groups and special events, and grant making through his family's foundation. He holds a Masters Degree in Social Entrepreneurship from Northwest University, and currently works with his wife, Colleen, in their restaurant, which they are building together to become "a commercial enterprise with charitable expressions." Jamie is the father of four grown children and grandfather of four, and resides in Bellingham, Washington.

FOREWORD

I wrote in the preface to the 20th anniversary edition of *A Long Obedience in the Same Direction,* "God doesn't change: He seeks and saves. And our response to God as He reveals Himself in Jesus doesn't change: we listen and follow. Or we don't. When we are dealing with the basics—God and our need for God—we are at bedrock. We start each day at the beginning with no frills."[1]

I wrote those words the same year Marvin Charles and his wife, Jeanett, launched a ministry to men helping them listen to and follow our Father, and be restored to their children. Marvin's book is the story of God and of the consequences of our listening and following—or not. It's a painful story of loss—the loss of a father and of fatherhood, the loss of dignity and hope, and the loss of character to addiction and indulgence. Sadly, it's a story repeated far too commonly throughout our history and our nation. Over 50% of African American children grow up in homes without their biological fathers and 39% of all school age children in America lack fathers at home. Millions live fatherless lives. The personal and social consequences of this are tragically documented in this book through Marvin's story.

Yet, it's also a beautiful story of being found—being found by our Heavenly Father, and being found by people of kindness and commitment who welcome the outcast. That, too, is a wonderfully repeated story throughout our history and our nation. It's a story worth repeating over and over. It's the story of the prodigal welcomed home.

In the story of being found, we also find the story of being reunited. In his reunion with God, Marvin also found his reunion with his seven children, and his never before known birth mother and birth father. This reunion is the story of God redeeming all things, and making all things new.

Marvin and Jeanett Charles have devoted their re-found lives to helping other men encounter the Father's love, and be reunited as fathers to their children. It's a story we need to hear and follow, for it's the story of God.

~*Eugene Peterson*
January 2016

PREFACE

I have had the privilege of knowing Marvin and Jeanett Charles since the year 2000, when we connected because of our common desire to advocate for committed fatherhood in the Seattle area. Our friendship grew stronger over the years as we raised our kids to see them launched into adulthood. We helped each other walk through some deep waters at different times of our friendship. Marvin and Jeanett blessed me by naming their youngest child after me, a beautiful girl named Jamie.

In the fall of 2012, Marvin and I sat having lunch at a Denny's restaurant off of I-405 in Bellevue, Washington, and I told him I was surprised that nobody had written his story yet. His reply was, "Why don't you help me do it?" For the next three years we worked on his story and on the D.A.D.S. story, in which Jeanett played a crucial part. In the process of Marvin recalling his journey, he gained valuable new insights into what God had led him through, and it bonded us closer together as friends.

After walking with Marvin for these past 15+ years, and even more closely these past four, I can confidently tell you that he is "the real deal"—and that being his friend is one of the greatest joys God has granted to me in this life. I sincerely hope you enjoy reading his story of becoming a responsible and committed dad. As God "reversed the curse" in his life, he has effectively been able help countless men do the same through the nonprofit Jeanett appropriately named "D.A.D.S." (Divine Alternatives for Dads Services).

Jamie Bohnett
Bellingham, Washington
January, 2016

TABLE OF CONTENTS

INTRODUCTION

Most child advocates agree that almost every social ill faced by America's children is related to fatherlessness. Children from fatherless homes are more likely to live in poverty, become involved in drug and alcohol abuse, drop out of school, and suffer from health and emotional problems. Boys are more likely to become involved in crime, and girls are more likely to become pregnant as teens.

In the United States today, more than 24 million children live in a home without the physical presence of a father. Millions more have dads who are physically present but emotionally absent. If fatherlessness were classified as a disease, it would no doubt be a certifiable epidemic worthy of attention as a national emergency.

If you are still not convinced, take a look at the statistics:

An estimated 24.7 million children (33%) live without the regular presence of their biological father.[2]

Of school-age children, 39% (17.7 million) live in homes absent their biological fathers.[3]

Breaking down the statistics further, 57.6% of black children, 31.2% of Hispanic children, and 20.7% of white children are living absent their biological fathers.[4]

Many people today do not understand why fatherlessness is such a threat to children and families. That's because we've been programmed to look at the symptoms of the problem—whether they be juvenile crime, unwed pregnancies, drug addiction, or gang violence—rather than the cause. I believe we need to take a more systemic approach.

When I speak to groups about the devastation that fatherlessness is causing in urban America, I equate it to the AIDS virus. AIDS doesn't kill in and of itself; what it does do is break down a person's immune system and make the individual susceptible to infections. Infections are what kill an AIDS victim. In the same way, a father's absence from the home opens up the family to all kinds of destruction, including the "symptoms" mentioned above.

We can point the finger all over the place at who or what is to blame for the current state of affairs. The reality is that it's a perfect storm of a number of factors, which I intend to illustrate in the coming chapters.

You Can Make a Difference
I realize there are several categories of people reading this book and I am grateful for the time and interest you are taking to do so. I want to address three particular segments of my audience:

1. You are a man in the situation described in this book. You have been outside the lives of your children and you want in. You are coming from some difficult circumstances and need advice on next steps to becoming an involved father in your children's lives. **You want help, support, and training.**

2. You are a person in the larger population who recognizes the devastating effects of fatherlessness in our society and in our nation. **You want to make a difference.**

3. You are employed in social work, the legal system, or a non-profit organization, and regularly work with families like those described in this book. You came into this field with a certain sense of idealism but since then you've seen a lot of discouraging situations. You may be disillusioned and calloused. **You want renewed vision and passion for your mission.**

Whichever category you fall into, I hope you take away from this book a renewed vision and practical tools for the road ahead. If each of us plays a part, we can all make a difference in the lives of our families and communities, and out of the rubble of broken lives and families, new life and hope can arise. There is a song that says it well:

> Yes, I will rise
> Out of these ashes rise
> From this trouble I have found
> And this rubble on the ground
> I will rise
> 'Cause He Who is in me
> Is greater than I will ever be
> And I will rise [5]

I believe we can turn our communities around by restoring fathers to their children. But in order to do that, we *must* reach absentee fathers with a message of hope and a vision for the future—as well as with practical support and resources. We also need to reach other corners of society and those working in the "system," educating people on what the real issues are that compromise families and energize the cycle of abandonment and fatherlessness. That is the mission of this book.

Since founding D.A.D.S. (Divine Alternatives for Dads Services) over fifteen years ago with my wife Jeanett, I have discovered that this elephant can only be eaten a bite at a time. That is, rather than wasting a lot of energy complaining about the current system, it is much more helpful to empower men to successfully navigate the system that already exists. We still advocate for reform of systems whenever possible. But, in the meantime, we can make great strides by empowering and equipping fathers in their dealings with "the system," and training and encouraging them to be strong, vital leaders in their families.

Many of those who have been involved with D.A.D.S. end up not only turning things around for themselves and their families, but discover a new life purpose. They see how their experience can be a platform for helping other men who are trying to overcome similar challenges.

One of my favorite verses in the Bible comes from the life of Joseph, when he finally revealed himself to his brothers who had callously left him in a desert well to die, "As for you, you meant evil against me, but God meant it for good, to bring about that many people should be kept alive as they are today" (Genesis 50:20). Whether the predicament in which a man finds himself as an "absentee father" is of his own making or the result of being born into a fatherless family, or a combination of both, every man still has a choice to turn to God and follow "divine alternatives," not only for the good of his children and their children, but also for other men in the community.

No matter how bleak a situation a man finds himself in, he can turn his life around and become a committed, involved father. The confidence I have about this is based upon the evidence of countless men—myself included—who have overcome many obstacles in order to build a better future for themselves and their children. Men who knew me in my former life, or who get a little glimpse of my story, will feel, *Wow! If this guy could turn things around, I sure can!* My story, which you will hear in the pages ahead, illustrates that "God doesn't call the qualified but rather qualifies the called."

As you read this book, it is my hope that you don't see this as "Marvin's story" or even "D.A.D.S.' story." I want you to understand the great dangers of fatherlessness in America, especially among low-income families. I want you to understand how the systems that have been put in place by well-intentioned govern-mental policies have made the problem of fatherlessness worse. When together we have an understanding of the real issues and their roots, we can begin as a community and as a nation to turn things around.

That is my hope. I hope you will join me in it.

"Being a father, to our own children or to someone else's,
or being something like a father
—an uncle, a mentor, a coach, a teacher, a therapist—
is the real way to become a man.
We gain our masculinity not by waving it from flagpoles
or measuring and testing it before cheering crowds
but by teaching it to boys and girls,
and to men and women who haven't known a man up close
and don't know what men and masculinity are all about.
If men would raise children,
it would not only save the world in a generation or two,
it would save their lives."

- Frank Pittman, *Man Enough*

CHAPTER ONE
Putting a Face on the Absent Father

The man stood outside on the street at midnight in Seattle, Washington, gulping down a 64-ounce can of malt liquor he had just bought at a convenience store with five bucks he had scrounged up. It was a cold, cloudless November night.

He looked up to the sky, where he could clearly see the moon. "Lord, I'm coming home." The words fell dully out of his mouth, more like a death wish than a hope for renewal. At 43 years old, his life was going nowhere and he didn't know what to do or where to go. He felt utterly lost and totally alone. As he wandered back into his girlfriend's apartment, he was greeted by what seeemed like all he ever heard now . . . more bad news.

"I'm pregnant again," she told him sadly. The man thought to himself, *One child was just born and now another baby is on its way?* He felt a sharp pain in the pit of his stomach. The only money coming in was the little bit he earned as a day laborer and the $1,000 or so he could get from a government tax refund check. What he had been thought of before as "always new"—going from job to job, smoking crack with his girlfriend to escape his pain—was getting really old.

He had six children scattered throughout the Seattle foster care system and elsewhere. Now there would be another, this one coming into a crack environment. Deep down, he knew they could not raise this child in any sort of healthy way.

He had started smoking crack regularly with his new girlfriend and her friends to make himself feel better, priding himself that he wasn't an "addict" like them—as if his drug use were under control. In reality he was just as trapped in addiction as they were. At the root, he was seeking to numb the pain he felt. His children were being raised by strangers. He was passing on to them, in all of their innocence, the very curse he had inherited. This cut him deeply to the core.

How had he come to this place? He was overwhelmed by the consequences of years of making bad choices that had seemed to make sense at the time. He felt trapped by single fatherhood and a doomed sense of unfulfilled responsibility. He was entangled in his addiction and the confusing web it had woven around his life and his identity. Now there seemed no way out. It felt like he was being sucked down a whirling funnel; it just spun faster and faster, dragging him into its vortex, and he was helpless to get out.

* * * * *

Nearly nine months later, the couple was sitting on the floor at a coffee table getting high on crack. The man suddenly noticed a puddle of what looked like water on the floor beside them. "What's that?" he asked.

"I don't know," his girlfriend replied flatly, as she continued smoking the crack pipe. She was oblivious to the fact that her water had broken and the baby was on its way.

Their daughter was born just as they reached the hospital. Amazingly, the medical personnel failed to run a drug test and after two days, the couple was released to bring her home. For the next seven months the pair continued smoking crack, regularly getting high with all of the madness that accompanied the lifestyle. The man took over as the baby's primary caregiver as his girlfriend was even deeper in her addiction than he was. He started to bond with this little girl through his daily care for her, even in his addicted state.

But as the cycle of addiction worsened, he knew they couldn't go on. One day he took the baby, grabbed a couple of cans of formula and four diapers, and left—with no plan of what he was going to do as he stepped out into the frigid morning air. It was December 22, 1997, three days before Christmas, but he couldn't care less. He knew there was no "Santa Claus fix" for the situation he was in.

He got off the bus at Harborview Medical Center, intending to leave the baby on the front steps of the hospital. He looked into her big brown eyes and started to cry. How had it come to this? *I'm 43 years old and this is what my life has come to? No job. No education. Six kids living in different places and now it will be seven. No hope at all. If hope cost fifty bucks I couldn't buy it because I wouldn't believe it was real.*

As he sat there in his misery and indecision, he tried the only thing he knew to do when he was really in trouble; he cried out, "God help me!" He had ignored God for years but who knew—maybe this time?

Just as he breathed out this desperate prayer he remembered a women's homeless shelter just around the corner. He walked there with the baby, hoping for some help. On his way down the steps to the shelter he spotted an empty, open backpack. "Thank you, God," he whispered. He dropped in the formula and the disposable diapers, put it over his shoulder, and carried the baby into the shelter. They kindly directed him to Child Protective Services and, although he hesitated, he realized he really had no other choice.

A CPS caseworker drove the man and child back to their apartment to get the necessary paperwork signed for relinquishment. When she opened the door, the man told his girlfriend abuptly, "We need to give the baby up to CPS." Reluctantly, she signed the paper. They walked back to the car and the father strapped the baby into her car seat and kissed her good-bye.

"Daddy's got to get it right. Daddy's going to see you again," he spoke gently to his baby girl. The caseworker closed the door and drove away.

As the car moved down the road he reflected on the unfairness of it all—not for him, but for his child. She didn't deserve any of this. She didn't deserve to be born with crack cocaine in her system. She didn't deserve to be raised in a drug environment or to suffer the consequences of her parents' choices. She didn't deserve to go from foster home to foster home and never feel the special love of a mom and dad.

The man loved his daugher and wanted to raise her with her mother. But if he was ever going to have that chance, he knew he needed to let her go . . . for now.

Real People, Real Stories, Real Barriers

This story is all too common, and the barriers facing this man, if he wants to get his daughter back, are almost unsurmountable:

1. He is addicted to crack cocaine, a habit that is even harder to break than addiction to heroin. Crack cocaine was this particular man's drug of choice, but many absent fathers turn to other drugs, some to alcohol. Once they begin to work with CPS, they can lose their children over a single glass of beer or glass of wine.

2. Chances are that this man has been in prison and prison is still in him. He knows he needs to get a job. If he has a record and if he is still using drugs he has little chance of being hired. He is stigmatized by his past.

3. He has tattoos from his time in prison. Many men in prison become tattooed with a distinctive kind of tattoo common to prison inmates. These tattoos can create an barrier for a man to be hired, as they can say to a potential employer: "ex-con."

4. Very likely he didn't have a father in his life, so he knows very little of what it means to be a committed father to his children. The "hidden tattoo" of fatherlessness can be even a greater barrier for a man to move ahead as a responsible, providing father.

5. He has lived an entire life of running from governmental authorities. In order for him to get his child back from the custody of the state, he will need to do the exact opposite of what he has done his entire life: submit to a host of authorities (Child

Protection Services (CPS), Division of Child Support (DCS), family court, the parole board, etc.) who will justifiably treat him with suspicion because of his past. They will not look kindly on him or "believe the best" about him. I once heard a DCS worker say, "We aren't social workers. We're bill collectors!" And to get his children back, a father will not just need to deal with these agencies once or twice; their often intrusive presence will continue in his life for years.

The obstacles he will need to cross over will seem endless, and every time he tries, a new obstacle will be before him. The temptation to quit this whole obstacle course over which he has no control is overwhelming.

Why can't this man just say, "I'm going to be a good father now and be involved in my children's lives," and get on with it? Maybe you yourself have looked at men like this and wondered, "Why can't they just step up to the plate and support their families?" It's much easier said than done. To understand, it is helpful to back up to the day the child is born to a mother who is part of the low-income community.

First, the mother and father are rarely married. Currently, 40.6% of all births in the US are to unmarried women. Breaking down that number by ethnic communities, the statistics are compelling: the out-of-wedlock rate for white women in 2014 was 29.3%. Hispanic women gave birth outside of marriage at a rate of 53.2%. And for African American women, the rate was 71.4%.[6] As a result, 57.6% of black children, 31.2% of Hispanic children, and 20.7% of white children are living absent their biological fathers.[7] Children from fatherless homes are more likely to be poor, become involved in drug and alcohol abuse, drop out of school, and suffer from health and emotional problems. Boys are more likely to become involved in crime, and girls are more likely to become pregnant as teens.

These are real people, real stories, and real obstacles.

How a "Deadbeat Dad" Is Made

Here's how it happens, more often than not: After the birth of her baby, a single mother will go down to the TANF (Temporary Aid for Needy Families) office to apply for governmental aid to enable her to raise her child. The father, in a proud moment at the hospital, is asked to sign a paper he thinks is the child's birth certificate. It is not. He is signing a promissory note agreeing to support this child's material welfare and to forego any DNA testing to determine the actual father. The information goes directly to the state Prosecutor's Office. Chances are the man will not see the letter, as he is a transient. If he can be contacted, he will likely choose not to open it because, "No good news comes out of the prosecutor's office!"

The federal government grants states the right to impute a wage on a man based upon his age and the assumption he is gainfully employed in a relatively high paying job. A schedule is imposed upon the man without his knowledge or consent, and the meter starts to run against him each month from the day his child is born. An "arrearage account" is established. It can add up to over $100,000 for most of these men within just a few years.

At some point, either while in prison or in rehab, a man has an "awakening" and wants to be a responsible father, to do the right thing. He goes out and gets a job. As soon as he gets that job his social security number is entered into the system. The government is ready to pounce now. This is the opportunity for the state to begin to recover the money that has been accumulating in the man's arrearage account. He is probably starting at minimum wage and as soon as he begins to work, the little bit of money he earns is taken away to reimburse the state. The only possible way for this man to survive is to return to his lifestyle "underground"—living under the radar, disconnected from his family, and probably engaging in a criminal lifestyle in some way. Not surprisingly, this man also has no place he can stay that would be available for a woman and her child or children. There are literally no men's shelters available where he can have a child with him.

What are the chances this man will ever be able to earn enough money to pay his astronomical back child support, secure decent housing, and support a family? Realistically, slim to none. How do I know?

Because the story at the beginning of this chapter is mine.

The Road to Recovery

I was at my very bottom when I watched my daughter Marvette being driven away from me that cold December day. I was 43 years old at that time. My wife Jeanett and I were both addicted to crack cocaine. But I wanted to change.

The first thing I needed to do was get into treatment, which I did a few months after that day. There, I became clean and sober and surrendered my life to Jesus Christ for Him to change my life from the mess it had become. And after that, I put the same energy I had put into living the fast life into doing whatever I needed to do to put Jeanett and myself into a position to get our family back together.

I was like a football team that was 0-16. Yet, little by little, I gained confidence: getting clean, taking parenting classes, helping Jeanett get into treatment, moving into transitional housing, finding a steady job, and renting a house. All this time, we were learning through trial and error how to successfully navigate the court system. We were learning first hand how hard it is to persevere through a system that isn't always "fair." We were also learning how to deal with the reaping of the consequences of our past foolishness.

It wasn't long before our children were able to come home and live with us. As this happened, a desire grew within us both to help other men to also find their way through the obstacle course of putting their families back together. In my case, I was given a more public platform as the story of my reunion with my birth mother after 43 years brought me recognition in Seattle through the newspaper and local television stations. It soon was picked up by ABC's *Good Morning America* and gave me an audience with public figures such as former Seattle Mayor Norm Rice.

But as we founded D.A.D.S. (Divine Alternatives for Dads Services) in 2000, we were also led to people of quiet inflence like Levi Fisher, who was strategically placed within the federal government, and Jamie Bohnett, who advocated involved fathering through his family's foundation. These men believed in us and what we wanted to do. They became early adopters and helpful connectors to others who made it possible to grow the D.A.D.S. organization that has impacted thousands of men in these past 16 years.

At D.A.D.S., we can encourage the men who walk through our door that there is hope—hope that perseverance will pay off in the end for them as they seek to be responsible fathers to their children. We can also point now to countless stories of men who have, like me, restored connection with their children. One by one, these men are fulfilling a scripture verse found at the very end of the Old Testament. The verse is hanging on the wall of our D.A.D.S. office. It reads, "And He will turn the hearts of the fathers to their children and children to their fathers" (Malachi 4:6).

There is hope for the absent father—I am living proof, as are thousands of other men who have walked through the doors of D.A.D.S. and found help, vision, and practical training for putting their lives and families back together. But there are thousands and thousands more who still need help. Fatherlessness is rampant in our nation, and I believe it is at the bottom of many if not most of our societal ills: Crime. Unwed pregnancy. Drug abuse. Sex trafficking. We fight these problems as singular issues but I believe there is a common root: fatherlessness.

There was no father in my mother's home. She was unprotected. She became pregnant. I was born without a father, and I grew up without the healthy protection of a father in my life and made many poor choices, as have many men like me.

I am grateful for the opportunities I have had to turn my life around. I look at my healthy, thriving family and think how easily it could have been a different ending. And my commitment is renewed to help fight fatherlessness and bring many more families to wholeness.

The tide can be turned. But much has to change in our communities and our nation, at a number of different levels, from the streets to the system. I am committed to helping make those changes in whatever ways I can. And that's the reason for this book.

So stay with me. But first I want to start at the beginning.

CHAPTER TWO
My Story Begins

I grew up as Marvin Louis Charles, the son of Mr. and Mrs. Edward and Nora Charles of Seattle, Washington, in an area now known as Martin Luther King Way. We lived there with my younger sister, Marion.

My father was a quiet man. I spent the most time with him on weekends, when he took side jobs cutting wealthy people's grass around Seattle, in places like Broadmoor and Mercer Island. During the week he worked as a sandblaster in West Seattle. He worked a swing shift, so he would come home after midnight completely dead tired. When he wasn't working, we would sit in front of the TV and watch shows like *Gunsmoke, Paladin,* and *Bonanza* together. Or, we would get dressed up—he in his Stetson hat, suit, and Stacy Adams shoes, and me in a little sailor suit—and head downtown. I remember feeling a strong sense of pride as I walked around with my dad, both of us looking so sharp. He did not read, write, or drive. We took the bus where we needed to go.

My mother, Nora Charles, was an outgoing and friendly woman who loved to go to church. She hosted what they called "missionary studies" in our house once a week. When she went to church, she would get decked out in her Sunday best and dress my sister and me "to the nines," too. Progressive Missionary Baptist, our home church, had been in our community for over fifty years. The church was an important, central part of our life.

My family always celebrated every holiday in a grand fashion. For Christmas one year, I received a red satin cowboy shirt with two six-guns, a rifle, a black suit, and some patent leather shoes. I was the sharpest looking cowboy in the West! And Thanksgiving was always a feast; the women in the family would cook for two days! Only later would I realize how much I would come to miss those happy times of extended family togetherness.

For summer outings, we all loaded up in the car and headed out to the Washington State coastline to dig for oysters and clams. Once, we got so many bags of oysters that the boat we were loading got stuck in the sand and mud! We had to wait until the tide came back in so we could move the boat back to the cars; it was so weighed down with our huge catch. These were some of my best memories.

But even as I approached the young age of seven, I began to lose some of the sweetness of my childhood. Losing innocence was not just about becoming exposed to sexuality too early; it also meant experiencing first hand the dangers of the neighborhood in which I lived. Empire Way was a busy street with constant traffic. The neighborhood was largely made up of African American families with some other ethnic groups mixed in. A family from India lived nearby, and a mixed race couple lived right next door. Five blocks down the road were Garfield High School and Horace Mann Elementary. We lived close enough to walk to and from school and my sister and I would come home for lunch each day. I felt safe in this neighborhood—until that feeling of security was taken away.

November 22, 1963, was a national loss of innocence. In school that day, teachers were crying and everyone was glued to the television. President Kennedy had been shot. This was incredibly tragic for my own community, as President Kennedy represented a sense of hope to the African American people. After Kennedy's assassination, I recall a feeling of increased or emphasized hunger for hope again in the African American community.

I believe it was partly out of this feeling that Motown became a force in the urban culture. The black entertainer was the first image I had of an African American being lifted up and admired in American society at large. Marvin Gaye, Tammy Terrell, Diana Ross, and Smokey Robinson were our new heroes. I remember my best friend and I putting on our fur hats, turning them backwards, and bursting out of the restroom of Horace Mann Elementary School singing the Beatles hit, "She Loves You," to a group of screaming and hollering girls. It felt good to be admired by the girls. The nation was going through traumatic times but I had sincere hope for my future. I was loved by my mom and dad, I was close to my sister, I was part of a tightly knit neighborhood, and I had extended family members who cared about me. But this was all about to change.

On April 15th, 1965, I woke up and started my day. I was nearly 10 years old. I brushed my teeth, got dressed, and readied myself for school. My mother, usually in the kitchen fixing Marion and me some breakfast, was not there that morning. Instead, she was laying on the couch, so we got ourselves some breakfast and headed out the door. When we came home for lunch, she was still on the couch, so we fended for ourselves and rustled up some lunch. When we returned home for the day at 3:30, she still had not moved. We figured out how to make ourselves dinner since our dad was at work.

The next morning, the same thing happened. My mother was never like this! I started to wonder if something was wrong with her. Maybe she was ill. When my sister and I returned home from school that afternoon, we found an ambulance parked outside of our house. My mother was taken away to the hospital. We watched it drive away, wondering to ourselves what we should do next.

Four days later, my Uncle E.J. and Aunt Helen came to the house. These two were not my favorite relatives. They were strict and stern and didn't seem to smile much. "Your mother has died and she was not your real mother and your father is not your real father," Uncle E.J. said to us matter of factly, hardly making eye contact. "You are now wards of the state but we will take you in. You are coming to live with us now." Nora Charles had died at the age of 47.

There would be no comforting of us by anyone. No explanation. No compassion for what we were going through. The funeral was five days later, on my tenth birthday. Not one person even said "Happy Birthday" to me. I looked at my father as we rode to the church, feeling confused and lost. I was in disbelief that this man was actually my adoptive father. Who was I? Where did I come from? No one had any answers for me.

A Whole New Life

The reception after the service was at Uncle E.J.'s house. He had three sons who were now grown and had left the house (except for the youngest who had returned from the Navy). I got a preview of what my life would soon be like living in the home of Uncle E.J. and Aunt Helen.

The people all seemed too happy to me, laughing when they should have been crying. Marion and I were all but ignored. One thing I remember was a conflict between Uncle E.J. and Aunt Mary on that very day. The conflict so upset Aunt Mary that she needed to be taken away from the home in an ambulance. In retrospect, I believe that Aunt Mary was "told" that Uncle E.J. would take us after the school year was finished. I believed there was some financial incentive involved for him doing this; this was money they could pocket from the Foster Care System.

For the rest of the school year, it was decided that we would stay with my Uncle Dave and Aunt Mary. These were my favorite relatives, as they had children near Marion's and my age. This was likely a practical matter as they lived near our school and it wouldn't necessitate us changing schools near the end of the school year. In June, we moved into Uncle E.J.'s house, where I shared the room with his adult son, Arthur, who was now in college.

That August, Uncle E.J. bought Aunt Helen a new 1965 Chrysler (possibly from extra funds he received for taking us in, in order to "sweeten the deal" for her). They took Marion and me and we drove to the Deep South with Aunt Helen to see Grandma Mary, who lived in Hammond, Louisiana. I recall the thunder and lightning storm that greeted us there. Grandma Mary's house had a tin roof and the rain beat above us relentlessly like a drum.

One day, we went into New Orleans and I spotted a drinking fountain and began to move towards it. Out of nowhere Grandma Mary smacked me right across my face, startling me. I later learned that I was attempting to drink from a "Whites Only" drinking fountain. At the time, we were on our way to the theater to watch a movie. After Grandma bought our tickets, we were taken to a back alley and walked up some rickety stairs that led into the balcony. As I looked below, I saw the lower level filled with white folks, while those in the balcony were all black. This was my first hand experience of the segregation that was still operating in the Deep South, even after the passing of the 1964 Civil Rights legislation.

As a young man, I just observed these things but nobody helped me understand or process them. I was truly feeling alone, part of a people who were seen as "less than" (particularly in certain parts of the country), and wondering who my real parents were. Were they still alive? Where did they live? I would not find out about them until many years later.

The Cold Years
At Uncle E.J.'s and Aunt Helen's, we were constantly corrected and "trained" to behave, to conform and act exactly how they wanted us to act. We heard no words of love, encouragement, or nurture—just rules. We were not to watch any television during the week, only on Saturday and Sunday afternoons. Although I was only in the fifth grade, I was to carry all of my books from school in my arms so I could do my homework, whether I needed to use all of my books or not. It was incredibly heavy to carry those books so many blocks each day, but I was not to leave a single book behind at school. Uncle E.J. would make sure of that.

Even though we went to a public school, Uncle E.J. made us wear Catholic uniforms to school every day. I wore salt and pepper slacks, a white dress shirt, and a blue sweater. I was teased mercilessly about the uniform by the other kids. I didn't dare question him, though, because everything was a one-way street and it only went his way. Homework was to be done strictly from 4 to 6 p.m.. Marion and I took turns, one week on and one week off, doing all of the dishes. Then it was upstairs to take a bath at 7:30 and by 8 p.m., we needed to be in bed.

The first taste of Uncle E.J.'s punishments came a few months into our stay with him. Marion and I were playing upstairs and I accidentally broke the window. I was scared to death of what my uncle would do. When I told him what had happened, he replied, "Go outside across the street and get a brick and two heavy rocks." He laid out newspaper on the hard ground in our front yard and made me crush the brick with one of the rocks. He then spread the crushed brick fragments over the newspaper and said, "Now kneel on the newspaper and hold up those rocks over your head." As I did this, he sat on a chair next to me with his belt, threatening to whip me if I lowered the rocks even an inch. I held them up for probably 15 or 20 minutes but it seemed like hours. My arms were aching from the weight of the rocks and my knees felt the sharp, unrelenting pain of the brick fragments piercing into my knees. My anxiety was amplified from the real fear of receiving a lash on my back, legs, or arms if I lowered the rocks above my head.

Uncle E.J. was also full of threats. In order to teach me to never steal, he held my hand over the red hot burner on the stove top. He told me, "If you ever steal, I will place your hand directly on this stove." Another time, he boiled several eggs in a pot. "If you ever lie to me, one of these scalding hot eggs will go in your mouth," he said to me. I was being terrorized with fear. I was scared to death that he would follow through with his threats so I never tested him to find out the answer.

"Pops" (my adoptive father) would occasionally stop in at the house—not to ever speak to us, but to drop by some fresh cows' mik that had not been homogenized. There would be huge gobs of curdled cream on the top and milky liquid on the bottom. We were made to eat the cream for breakfast. It was disgusting, but Aunt Helen forced us to eat it before we went to school. We had never been forced to eat anything before by my mother, but with the scary presence of an ever-angry Uncle E.J. lurking in the background, we just gulped it down.

I began to "live in my head," keeping my thoughts and feelings to myself. It was my way to try to adapt and survive. I felt like a little puppet. I would have done anything to experience even a taste of freedom.

"I've had enough of you," Uncle E.J. suddenly announced one day. "You're going to live with your dad for a while." So, that summer I was sent there and Marion went to stay with a lady who had been a friend of my mom's. My dad rented a house with a man who was a pimp, although that didn't mean much to me as I didn't really know what that signified. During this time period, Washington was a loose place in this regard. Rosellini was governor and laws about prostitution were lax in enforcement as military personnel provided a very willing clientele.

Pops' roommate drove a T-Bird and wore slick clothes. Pops lived the straight life and got no respect from others, mockingly refered to as "Mule" by his friends and acquaintances. He made enough money to pay his rent but little else.

I didn't respect or fear my dad. His roommate, on the other hand, seemed to live a much more interesting and affluent lifestyle—in my eyes, at least.

Pops never gave me money, so I found "creative" ways to get what I wanted. I began to steal things like clothing and shoes. While at my father's house, I remember seeing strong images of men that I wanted to be like when I grew up, but they weren't my dad. These images were reinforced by films like *Super Fly* and *Shaft*, films that portrayed African American men who were heroes in the ghetto—tough, street-smart, and able to take care of themselves and attract beautiful ladies. This was also a time of the rise of Motown entertainers like Isaac Hayes, Marvin Gaye, and Smokey Robinson. They painted a picture for me of what it looked like to be a successful black man as the 1970s approached and I moved into adolescence. With no father to really look up to and admire, these guys were my role models.

Once, while sitting on the porch at my Pops' place, I saw a dude named Sammy Drain. He wore a loud, red sharkskin suit. Attached to him were two poodles dyed different colors. His processed hair was slicked down like James Brown. I was captivated by him. Later, I observed another cat pulling up across the street in his canary yellow, half-cap 1968 El Dorado. He stepped out with a mink fur coat and a hat to match. I saw him pick up his clothes from the cleaners and throw them into his trunk and spin out from the parking lot. He was bent over, with one hand on the wheel. This impression was seared into my mind. I wanted to be like that cat!

Around age 13, I began to envy the kids whose parents were in "the Game," which is what everyone called the pimping and prostitution industry. Those kids had the freedom I longed to have. They were preparing themselves to become "players" themselves someday by honing their salesmanship skills selling candy door-to-door for a couple of older, up-and-coming players. These older boys made some money off the younger kids as a means for a "come up," which allowed them to purchase the items they needed to make them look like pimps (or "players.") They were like minor league pimps. I tried selling, but I wasn't any good at it. I was considered a "square" by those who wanted to come up. I was at the bottom of the bottom of the food chain.

To my disappointment, I had to return to my uncle and aunt's house after two years of living with Pops. Sure, I wasn't living high on the hog at Pops' house, but I had freedom. My clothes (which are really important to a middle school kid) were either stolen or picked up at the Navy surplus store, and I liked them. My hair had grown out into an Afro style. But coming back to my uncle's house, that all ended. The hair was shaved short. Uncle made me wear again, now in ninth grade, that terrible Catholic uniform. It had felt humiliating in seventh grade and was now even more so in the ninth. Marion and I both had to be in bed by 8 p.m. again. It was all the same rules but this time it felt doubly miserable. I had tasted the hip culture of the late sixties in Seattle and being back at my uncle's house felt like prison.

I had gradually outgrown the asthma that had plagued me as a child, so now I was finally able play sports like basketball and football. I was a legend in my own mind. My pride was bolstered after I made a half court shot one day on the basketball court. I just knew I would be famous someday.

I was embarrassed to be called Marvin Charles, after my dad, so I came up with a fantasy name that sounded real cool, "Brooklyn Taylor." I practiced signing autographs. At this time, I had no guidance or help of any involved adult, like an engaged father, who could show me what actual steps I needed to take in order to make my dreams into an honorable reality. All I had were my dreams, and misguided ones at that.

Steps in the Wrong Direction
It was now the spring of 1969 and I was playing basketball with a guy at school. I asked him if I could wear his jean jacket to the lunch room, where I was spotted by an upperclassman who thought I had stolen the jacket. Without warning, he smacked me in the jaw. I walked away, but not to walk away from a fight. I was getting a weapon. I gave a smaller kid some change and told him to buy me a Coke. When he returned with it, I poured out the contents and smashed the bottom, leaving a jagged, sharp edge. I was fighting for my reputation! I started out towards the young man who hit me and felt someone grab me from behind. Instinctively, I wrestled with this other person, accidentally cutting him on his eyebrow. Turned out, it was the school's principal.

Now I heard the kids clapping, believing I had purposely cut the principal. This was a time when it was particularly "cool" for youth to rebel against authority. Bleeding, the strong African American man grabbed me by my shirt, trying to stop the blood from oozing out of the wound near his eye as he walked me to his office. When I got out of sight from the other students, I began to wail in remorse over what had occurred. I was filled with indignation at being falsely accused of stealing and then being cold-cocked. Even though this was an accident, I had in fact assaulted the principal. As a result, I was suspended from Seattle public schools. When the following school year started, I was re-admitted and permitted to attend Ingraham High School in North Seattle, one of only three black kids in the entire school.

One day, in tenth, grade, I lost my house key and asked Marion to leave her key under the mat so I could get inside. Uncle E.J. found out and made her put the key under the mat as if nothing was wrong. When I walked into the house, he was right there. He told me to get naked, then demanded I go outside and get a brick from across the street and two large rocks, like before.

I ran outside, but this time I had no intention of ever returning. When I was two blocks away, I realized I just couldn't leave my sister behind. I ran back to the house to find her sobbing uncontrollably. "Come with me; you've gotta get out of here. This man is crazy," I appealed to her.

"I can't, Marvin, I can't," she responded brokenly. I decided to leave anyway, and walked straight to the Youth Detention Center. I now knew I needed to go to court for my freedom and face the self-righteous anger of Uncle E.J. head on.

"I never thought you would do this to us," my aunt said to me as we were sitting next to each other in the courtroom. I proceeded to detail to the judge some of the things Uncle E.J. had done to Marion and me since we had been in his home.

The judge patiently listened and then turned to my uncle and said, "Did you do these things?"

Uncle E.J. unapologetically and defiantly exclaimed, "If he is going to live in my house, he is going to have to live by my rules."

The judge was not impressed with my uncle's answer. With the swing of his gavel, he declared, "I am hereby making this child a ward of the state."

I didn't look them in the eye. I was glad to not have my uncle tormenting me anymore. I was greatly relieved I didn't have to see his face anymore. But what now?

CHAPTER THREE
A Pivotal Year

Garfield High School in Seattle in the early 1970s was known as "the Dog House." It was the place you wanted to go to if you lived in the hood. It seemed like greatness came out of that school. Because of the intentional racial integration through bussing in the 1960s in Seattle, I attended an almost all-white Ingraham High School in North Seattle. Nearby Garfield High School was the school that spawned such legends as Jimi Hendrix, Bruce Lee, and Quincy Jones. Almost all of the kids in the hood went to either Garfield or Franklin. Garfield was where the action was and that's where I wanted to be. I hated being in almost all-white Ingraham High School. "I want to be back in the hood. I want to be around black folks where I won't be singled out," I explained to my guidance counselor. They allowed me to transfer for my senior year to Garfield. Little did I know that this year at Garfield, becoming a Bulldog, being in "the Dog House" would change my life for years to come. Being able to attend

Garfield was like a reunion. I reconnected with kids I hadn't seen since elementary and middle school. At the time, it had two campuses, the "A" campus, which was the main building on Jefferson Street, and the "B" campus on Jackson Street. We went back and forth between the different campuses.

I no longer had to wear the Catholic uniform and needed a bit of a wardrobe update. I was pretty much cured of shoplifting by this time, so I decided to get a job to earn money for some better clothes. I signed on at the Neighborhood Youth Corps for an after school job for about two and a half hours, five days a week, at Madrona Elementary, not too far from Garfield and only six blocks from where I lived. My job was to sweep out the rooms and empty the trash for about $23 a week. This was enough to buy me some new shoes and pants occasionally.

Things had really changed for me now. Before, I had been on the outer edges of the hood, attending a nearly all-white school in north Seattle. Now I was in the "cool school." I had a little job where I could earn some cash and I had no curfew. I was now living in my friend Teddy's house. His mother, an elderly woman, really had little control over the house. It was more of a place where you would just come and go, like a pit stop. As I began living in this home, I carried over habits I learned from living at my uncle and aunt's house. For example, I was the only one who cleaned up after myself or did the dishes. The others in the home made fun of me for obeying rather than ignoring Teddy's mother.

That spring, Teddy and a group of young guys my age (16 to 17 years old) went with Bobby Green, who was about 21, to Spokane to sell candy. Bobby was an entrepreneur who had a nice car and a girlfriend. All ten or eleven of us piled into a U-Haul truck and headed east about 300 miles to Spokane. He handed us maps of the area we were to cover, and we sold candy all day. I hadn't done very well at selling candy before, and as I tried this time I wasn't much better at it. The ones who did do well got to sleep in the hotel room with Bobby. The ones who didn't do so well slept in the truck. Needless to say, I slept in the truck.

One morning, a big commotion arose among Bobby and the boys who slept in the room. Teddy was among them. Some money had been taken from Ricky. I knew it was Teddy, as I had dealt with him in the home; he had stolen from his mother and me, and had falsely accused me of stealing. I approached Bobby and told him who I believed did the stealing. Then I went to Ricky and challenged him, "These guys are your friends. Why didn't they stick up for you and tell Bobby that Teddy had ripped you off?" Teddy never "fessed up" but they were able to get the money together to pay Ricky back. But from this point on Ricky and I became close friends. He knew I had his back.

After that trip, Ricky invited me to his home, where I met his mom and dad, and they eventually invited me to live with them. Their place felt like a real home, something close to what I experienced before my mom had died and I was abruptly taken from that place of security. Ricky and I were now best friends, heading into the summer before my senior year. We hung out and smoked a little pot as summer turned to fall. I was really looking forward to the school year and my focus now was on the girls. As I would say, "Garfield had some lacks but it also had some max." One of them was a girl named Barbara. She was beautiful. (Sadly, I later found out that she wound up as a centerfold for Playboy in 1977, became addicted to heroin, and tragically committed suicide by jumping off the Highway 99 bridge in Seattle.)

As my senior year began, I was disappointed that the

basketball coaches didn't seem to want me. I was 6' 2" and could with one hand dunk the ball, but I felt I didn't get a good look. They cut me. After being a starter at Ingraham, this was humiliating. I needed to find another way than sports to make my mark. So, I began to dress slick. Ricky got his driver's license and could use his parents' car, so I went with him to parties in the city, dressing cool to try to attract the girls.

One day, I was hanging out in the hallway and a girl came up and said she was taking sign ups for "Mr. Bulldog." This was a competition that determined the "king" and "queen" of the school, that culminated with a big limousine ride down 23rd Avenue. I liked the sound of it, and signed up to join the competition. Until then, "Mr. Bulldog" was something that was given to the most popular dude on campus; it wasn't something you campaigned for. I changed all of that. I talked to the girls—especially the underclass girls, freshmen, sophomores, and juniors— and asked them to vote for me. "Vote for me and Yvette Hunter," I told them with a smile.

As the day of the announcement was going to be made, David Barfield, a security guard and an alumni of the school came up to me and teased, "Hey man, I know who won Mr. Bulldog." I couldn't tell if he was talking about me or he was just clowning me, knowing it was someone else.

When I found out that the announcement of the winners was going to be made I quickly went home and changed clothes. I put on some blue suede shoes, lime green slacks, a white blazer, and a Robin Hood hat. At the assembly in the gym, a faculty member made the announcement, " . . . and Mr. Bulldog and Mrs. Bulldog for 1973 are . . . Marvin Charles and Yvette Hunter!" Suddenly the crowd started pounding their feet in the bleachers and bellowing out loud "boos." A few faint cheers could be heard from some underclassmen but the boos drowned them out. I felt a strange mixture of elation and humiliation. I felt the satisfaction of accomplishing something I wanted, to be "Mr. Bulldog" through my powers of persuasion, but I also felt rejection from my peers who seemed to be saying to me, *You don't belong. Who are you, Marvin Charles? You aren't one of us. You don't deserve to be "Mr. Bulldog."* And that feeling of not belonging, not fitting in, felt awfully familiar.

I shook off that feeling and tried to take in the fleeting glory that a Mr. Bulldog gets to have, as photos were taken of Yvette Hunter and me. Later, that Friday night, was the Homecoming Game at Memorial Stadium near the Space Needle in downtown Seattle. Keith Harrell, a basketball star and marching band leader, formed the band around Yvette and me. The next day, Saturday, we stood on a float and waved at the crowd at the parade.

It was the following Monday when I was called into the principal's office. His words were blunt, "Marvin, you aren't setting a good enough example as Mr. Bulldog." He proceeded to tell me that I didn't have enough credits to graduate. He told me I had only 23 credits that year and supposedly needed 55. Later I learned that I only needed 24, so was in actuality only one credit short. These are the kinds of situations where a parent can exert strong influence and help but I didn't have that. All I could see was that I was being perceived in a negative light. I was thinking, *What am I doing wrong? I am dressing pretty slick, selling a little weed (that they don't know about); I'm not doing anything too blatantly wrong. Why am I always being singled out as being trouble?* It was spring and I was so close to graduating from high school, yet I was so far.

BECOMING DADS

About that time, Ricky got into a squabble with his parents. "I'm running away from home. Do you want to come with me?" he asked. I agreed and we went to Bellingham, near the Western Washington University campus, about 90 miles north of Seattle, where my Pops lived, now remarried. But before long, Ricky's mother, Emma Cotton, found Ricky and me. Ricky was taken away by the police, as he was under age, and put in Juvenile Hall. I had just turned 18, and had nowhere to go.

"You stay away from my son," Mr. Cotton warned me sternly as he backed me up against the railing outside of the apartment. I thought to myself, *This angry man is going to push me off this balcony!*

Depressed, with no place to go, I caught a ride back down to Seattle, now homeless, but not for long. When Ricky was let out of Juvenile Hall he found me and we moved in with his grandmother. This house had rats that kept me awake at night.

I started to feel like I had some kind of disease that others wanted to avoid. Parents wanted to keep me away from their kids. I wasn't going to graduate now with my classmates. I could hear the voices, "Ricky was a good kid until he met you, Marvin."

I could hear the condemning voice of my Uncle E.J., always telling me that I would amount to no good, and Uncle Dave telling me I couldn't come back to his home. I could hear Pops' voice accusing me of being a thief; I could remember Mr. Bass, the Garfield principal, telling me I wasn't setting a good enough example as "Mr. Bulldog." I could hear them all saying I was no good. I sat on the curb of 23rd and Cherry and cried, "I never asked for any of this!"

"Well then, I may as well be about it," I said to myself one day (being "about it" means being a part of the Game). By saying this out loud, a weight seemed to be lifted from my shoulders. What I was really shouting in my soul was, *I don't need to fight this anymore. I'm on the devil's team.* I could feel a strange peace come over me as I asserted this out loud. A war seemed to be over. They were all right. Everyone around me saw what I didn't want to see. Now I could clearly see it. I now knew deep down what they all had been saying to me all along. I belonged to the dark side. I was going to join the Game.

BECOMING DADS

CHAPTER FOUR
Life on the Dark Side

My opportunity came one day when I was hanging around with Ricky. Down the street came "L.A. Slim," driving a blue Gran Torino with a white top. He stopped his car and said to me, "I've got a ride to Canada. Get you a girl and you can ride with me." I knew what he was saying without saying more. He was going to Canada where prostitution was legal, to do some pimping. He was inviting me into the Game.

I went back to my friend's house and started what they call "talking trash" to a girl named Wanda who wanted to go and do some hustling up north. We joined L.A. Slim, drove up to Canada, and checked the girls into a couple of cheap hotel rooms. The thing to do was to drop the girls off, make sure they were settled, and then leave them to do their business. To hang out and do more was known as "micro-managing" and that was not professional conduct in the Game.

A week later, Wanda popped in and handed me a wad of about $300 in cash. Now I had a taste of being in the Game and saw the way it worked. Real money could be made with very little effort on my part. I bought a real nice *Super Fly* suit with that cash.

After the summer, I had to find another place to live. This constant search for a place to sleep was becoming part of my life now. My lack of parental support was always just below the surface in my mind. I thought back frequently on all the times I had been told I wasn't good enough—that to Uncle E.J. and Aunt Helen, my sister and I were second-class citizens. Not even my Pops wanted me. My friends' parents said I was a bad influence. School teachers and counselors didn't believe in me. I felt that all of these perceptions painted the true picture of who I really was.

The stress must have been gettting to me, because soon I began having terrible headaches, so bad that I went to the hospital one day. It was there that Miss Colacerto (I would later call her my "angel"), picked me up and said to me, "You need to get your high school diploma, Marvin. As long as you do something productive you can stay with me." I attended Langston Hughes Alernative School for the next six months to get enough credits to graduate. The proudest moment of my life was walking across that stage and graduating from high school.

Miss Colacerto helped me get my first real job, working for Unigard Insurance Company on Capitol Hill in the mail room. The reason I took the job was that after six months of working there, I knew I could qualify for a loan to get my first car. I had my car, the clothes, and I knew how to play the Game. I was now ready to make some real money pimping.

Learning about Life in "the Game"

First of all, I needed to get my "props and tools." I had to get that car, as that was the most important tool I needed. The job would make it possible for me to get a loan; if I worked there for at least six months then I could qualify, and I could get my car.

Around this time I met a young hooker named Laura. I wasn't involved with her, but she gave me $300 so she could crash at my pad with her baby. When she did her tricks she took the baby to stay with a relative. I took the money and bought an "eight ball" of cocaine (about an eighth of an ounce) from Uncle Todd, cut it up, and divided it up into 20 packets. I needed to cut the cocaine and asked for his advice. He told me to go to the drug store and buy some "Dormins" (a sleep aid) there. Little did I know that he was sabotaging me to teach me a lesson, and to discourage me from selling the drug in the future.

What I should have used was a lactose that would only dilute the cocaine but not take it over and give the user a painful, burning sensation in the nostrils. I took it down to the corner to test it out and sold it to some younger kids. "What's this #&$!! cut with?" demanded one of the punks. I tried it and my nostrils burned.

I thought angrily to myself, *Uncle Todd has done it again!* He always seemed to be trying to teach Ricky and me a lesson.

One time, Ricky and I stole some of Uncle Todd's guns and worked up the nerve to go to an after-hour club (clubs that would open after 2 p.m. for gambling, dope dealing, using, and prostitution). We drove there in Ricky's Cadillac, dressed to the nines and packing Uncle Todd's "borrowed" guns. We strolled in, sat at the bar, and ordered a couple of rum and cokes. We were scouting women for the Game.

That night the police raided the club. The uniformed officers walked in calmly and made us line up against the wall. They frisked and searched us (men and women both), took our cash, confiscated our weapons, photographed us, and checked our names for warrants. "You can pick up your money and guns at the station," they said to us sarcastically, knowing that most of us would never go within a mile of the station. Uncle Todd had to go and retrieve his registered guns from the police.

The next time I saw him, he told me, "Marvin, they've got a picture of you down at the police station standing on Madison, handing something to somebody. They can prove you were selling drugs." He was lying to me; I had never sold dope on Madison. He was trying to scare me away from dope dealing, just as he had been doing when he told me to cut the cocaine with Dormins.

Uncle Todd was for the most part a "square" (what we called those who made their money legally). He didn't want Ricky (his nephew) or me (his "adopted" nephew) to do what we were doing. He worked with the pipefitters' union and was a member of "Project Mister," a group of black businessmen in the Seattle area who sought to mentor at-risk minority youth, mainly African-American. He really did have our best interests at heart.

I was still going to work daily for Unigard when Laura suddenly left. I had hidden my cocaine, knowing she may come back for some. One night, I heard a hard knock on the door; it was Laura and her pimp, Joe B., with a gun. I climbed out the window and ran to a friend's house. The door was unlocked so they walked right in and rummaged through my stuff, looking for the cocaine I had hidden. They didn't find it but when I got home I found a framed photo of me and a girl with a bullet hole through it, and shattered glass on the floor all around it. A note was attached to it that said, "Stay away from my broad." Joe B. was teaching a lesson to Laura and to me. Message received.

Joe B. knew the $300 Laura had given me was "his money," and he wanted it back. In the Game, 100 percent of the money earned on the street goes to the pimp, to be redistributed at *his* discretion. Laura had violated the rules and I was sure she'd been beaten for that. Joe B.'s willingness to enforce the rules with a gun was all part of the mind control of pimp over prostitute in the Game. I was quickly learning how to play that Game, and this was all part of my "continuing education."

"I have to get out of this shotgun apartment," I thought to myself. I found out that around the corner, the landlord was offering a place for $135 a month, a little more than my $90 apartment. It needed furniture, so I went to the furniture store with the cash I'd earned from my job. But it was too much; I couldn't afford the furniture without a loan, and to get a loan I needed a co-signer, but I had nobody to co-sign for me.

It was a constant cycle. Everything seemed be learned from hitting my head against a wall. All the disjointed pieces of my identity—of not belonging to anyone, of being no good, a bad influence, a negative example to others—all lined up to paint for me an undeniable picture of who I really was. Reluctantly, I now started to believe it. I should go ahead and live my life from my true identity. The square way would never work for me because that's not who I was. Besides, the square life wasn't moving fast enough for me.

So there I was, in my late teens. I knew I didn't want to sell dope as my main money source. In the hood, a lot of young African American men over 18 were sent to prison for selling drugs. I also didn't want to have to steal. No matter how good you were at that, it eventually got you to prison. Pimping, the fast life, the Game, were what I thought would provide the best chance for me to make good money and stay out of prison. By the six-month mark of my working at Unigard, I was able to secure a $2,000 loan so I could buy a car. I quit my job one week later.

Getting Serious

Having a car at 19 was huge for me. But now, with no job, I needed to get myself busy and try to find a girl or two to put to work for me. I needed to get serious about developing my new profession. So, Ricky and I drove down to Portland looking for girls, since Portland had a "track" (a street where prostitution takes place).

What followed was an endless ebb and flow of different hookers, different cars, different hotels, different cities. In order to make the most money and stay in the best position possible in the Game, I was in contant flux. Seattle to Oakland, Oakland to Portland, San Francisco to Phoenix, and even down south to San Diego. We'd head over to Spokane, Yakima, and back to Seattle for a while. Girls would choose me or I would "knock them" from other pimps, and then eventually they would leave (get pregnant, get arrested, get knocked by other pimps, run away, etc.). With some I would form close bonds and they would stick around for years.

At the same time, I was feeling jealous of what Ricky had. He was pressured by his parents to put his money into buying a house. He then flipped his car to buy a 1973 El Dorado. Even if he was controlled a little by his parents, he at least had family support with two parents who cared for him. He was able to get co-signatures on loans. He seemed to always stay a step ahead of me because he had the "crutches" I didn't have. I felt all alone in the world. This loneliness and envy I felt was just adding gasoline to the fire of my desire for a "normal" family in my life. I believe I was trying to recreate my lost family through attracting girls to work for me and by spending time learning the Game from more experienced players over a bowl of cocaine. It was substitute family.

In November of 1975, I met Herb, a man whom others refered to as "Superb Herb." He was a jolly older pimp who knew everybody and everybody knew him. He described Fresno as "the Promised Land" of prostitution. Fresno was an agricultural area with a large Hispanic worker population and police who, for the most part, looked the other way. I thought he took some kind of pride in taking me under his wing. He saw my potential as a pimp and treated me with a kind of fatherly concern I hungered for.

When we arrived in Fresno, he introduced me to some other pimps who all had six or seven girls and their own nice, comfortable places to live. I now saw the Game from a whole different perspective. These guys were different from the pimps I had known in Seattle. They blended into the square world. They were almost "conservative." We went out and had a "blow" together while our girls were working. We would sniff cocaine for hours. Things were looking up again for me—or so I thought.

By 1978, I was back in Seattle. During this time, I did something that meant a lot to me. I drove over the same place that, as a 14-year old boy, I would sit and people watch. Then, it was a drycleaner and I was watching the pimp George T. walk out of the cleaners to his yellow and brown '68 El Dorado and drive away with style. Now, at 24, I drove to the same spot, now a restaurant, in my '78 El Dorado. I stepped out of my car in my sharkskin two-piece suit, stiched in black with my initials embroidered on it. My hair was relaxed back like his was. I ordered a meal to go, and as I got into my car I remembered how George had dropped his steering wheel into his lap and peeled off. I did the same thing, bent over the wheel just like him, handling it with just one hand. I drove off with a personal sense of accomplishment. I was George T., the 1978 version.

By 1979, I had four girls. We headed over to Virginia and then later D.C.. I was finally in a place that Ricky hadn't been in. In the back of my mind, I was always competing with him. I loved being on the East Coast. It was here I was exposed for the first time to free basing cocaine. (That's when it is put into a test tube, with a couple drops of ether, then separated before being scraped up into a light powder and smoked.) This was a purer, more powerful form of cocaine. In D.C. I was now beginning to feel respected. One pimp said to me, "Man, you gotta be one helluva nigga coming all the way from the West Coast." The 1980s were coming and, to me, the future was lookin' bright.

By January of 1980, we were back on the West Coast. I had taken a couple of my girls to a fancy night club in San Fransico to celebrate New Year's Eve. One of my girls, Gay, was known to get a little out of hand when she started drinking. I did not want her to disrespect me in public, in front of these other well-known pimps and big leaders in the Game, so I was apprehensive about letting her drink. She said to me, "Hey baby, order me a fifth of Black Velvet whiskey." I was torn, but eventually decided that it couldn't hurt. *She's made me a lot and she earns it,* I thought. Big mistake.

Gay started to act "loose"—becoming sexually suggestive—then started loudly arguing with one of my other girls at our table. I had had enough. I grabbed her arm harshly and walked her outside. I dragged her down the stairs, opened the trunk of my car, and bundled her inside, slamming it closed. I then calmly buttoned up my suit coat and walked back upstairs to sit down with my other girls. I felt no remorse.

Making the two-hour drive back to our home with Gay in the trunk, I thought to myself, *I've worked too hard to let some drunk broad take down my reputation.* I felt nothing for Gay, who was hurt and bleeding in the trunk of the car. I pretended she wasn't even there. When we pulled into our place in Salinas, California, I popped the trunk to let her out and she moaned half-coherently, "I can't move my arms." I'm sad to say, I still felt no remorse. My heart was cold.

It was now 1982 and I went to a player's party in Seattle. I felt like I was returning a huge success. People knew who I was and what I was doing. I was now rolling five deep with five hookers. *I've made it. I am no longer that 16-year-old kid who walked the streets of Seattle on the outside looking in,* I thought to myself. *I'm an international pimp now with all of the cars, jewelry, and clothes I want. My name is ringing across the country.* It was during this time that I let myself really indulge in crack for the first time. I felt I deserved the celebration. I started seriously smoking. I couldn't stop, and stayed awake for over three days.

Deeper and Darker
Later, the girls and I headed to Florida. One night, one of them came back from the bar without my money and started to take a shower. I yelled out at her, "Ain't you supposed to be getting ready to work?"

She responded, "I'll get ready when I want to get ready." I couldn't tolerate that kind of disprespect, and pulled her out of the bathroom. When I finally released my grip for a moment, she broke for the door and burst out of the hotel room, running down the hallway completely naked. Here I was, a black man in the Deep South, with a naked white woman screaming and running away from me.

I quickly put on some pants and grabbed a briefcase full of jewelry and walked past the hotel residents who were now staring at me. I then slipped out the door, broke across a field, and disappeared into the night without any shirt or shoes. I found myself walking in the dark, alligator-infested woods. I got tired of walking and started to wonder if my next step would be a chomp from a gator. I decided to head back to the hotel to see if it was safe to go back to the room. I crawled up to the grassy area outside of the parking lot and came within about 100 yards of my car, which had a police car parked right next to it! I quickly decided to take Orange Blossom Trail instead, the main road that connected Kissimmee to Orlando. As I was walking down that street, I spotted a parked car that suddenly turned on its lights. The police had spotted the shirtless, shoeless black man they had been looking for. The chase was over.

They put handcuffs on me. I heard one of the officers say, "I think we have our suspect." Then the same policeman turned to me and said, "Buddy, you're going to prison." They booked me and sent me back to jail. Before I knew it I was in dress down blues.

After 30 days in jail, I was transferred to the downtown jail. I was now getting scared. All the "hard core" criminals were there. Several of them took me under their wing, and it was in jail that I formed some connections with criminals who would probably be there for life. Unexpectantly, the prostitute who started the whole jail experience came to visit me. "I'm leaving, but I don't want to press charges. I thought you should know that." Walking back to my cell, I knew that this was good news. I should be getting out soon.

Shortly afterward I was released from jail, after seven months of being locked up. As I exited the building, I put on a tee shirt and tennis shoes and walked only a block before I bought an "eight-ball" of dope. I locked myself in a motel for three days and ran through about $600 dollars of drugs. It was now 1986 and my cocaine use was increasing. I had been able to control it in the past, but now it was starting to control me. I was getting worried—although I wasn't ready yet to do anything about it.

BECOMING DADS

CHAPTER FIVE
Unplanned Fatherhood

Around this time, I found out that Rhonda, one of my girls, was pregnant with my child. She had had two or three abortions previously, but this was the first pregnancy she decided to keep, thinking it was time to have a family of her own. How did I feel about her being pregnant? Rhonda had been committed and loyal to me; I felt I owed it to her to be equally committed to her. So, I chose to support her.

On July 13th of 1987, Rhonda gave birth to our son, Nick, six weeks prematurely. Nick was in an incubator for the first four days of his life but was able to come home from the hospital with Rhonda. Just a couple of weeks later, she was back at work. She found a family to watch Nick while she worked the streets.

When I got back to California, I found out I had fathered another son by one of my other girls; she had named him Dontay. He had been born thirteen months before Nick, although I hadn't known about him. I didn't want to get caught up in his mother's drama, so I would just pop my head in and out occasionally to see my son. I was quickly realizing that I wasn't able to be the kind of father I wanted to be.

It was now 1988, and I was getting high in a dope house in Salinas when I met Kathy, a pretty black prostitute who was also an expert thief. Rhonda was adjusting to motherhood. Kathy was a money maker. Between thievery and turning tricks, she got enough cash for us to go to Montana, Salt Lake City, and Reno. Things were getting increasingly more complicated. My dope use was increasing and in 1989 Kathy became pregnant with our child. All of these babies were my children. How could I make this work?

One day, when she was almost five months pregnant, Kathy's thievery brought in $10,000. At this point, we decided she needed to get an abortion, as she was our main source of money. We needed her to keep working! On the way to her abortion appointment, we got high and forgot about it. We moved to Montana, where Kathy had the baby, and we named him Marvin Junior. Although I didn't recognize it at the time, God's grace was very present, even in my darkened state.

It was at this time that crack cocaine was introduced in Billings. The effects were catastrophic. Prostitutes and pimps alike quickly became addicted, and the money from that industry was siphoned off by the drug dealers and re-routed back to California. The underworld economy was devastated.

As a result, money was scarce the next three years. When it dried up, I sold all of our furniture and Kathy and I and baby Marvin moved into a motel room. I bought a car, but never got the plates; I only had a temporary sticker. Life was difficult. Kathy and

I fought frequently and she eventually fled my anger and abuse—and I didn't see her and Marvin Jr. again for several months.

I drove to Spokane, Washington, looking for a way to hustle myself back to California where Rhonda and Nick were. It was here that I met Carol. I made my way to Seattle, trying to "come up"—which in street vernacular means I was trying to gather a stable of girls to work for me again. I fell in and out of contact with some other prostitutes from my past, having relationships with some of them. I finally wound up again in California, at what was probably my lowest point ever.

Rhonda was in another committed relationship now, so I had limited access to my son Nick. Kathy was out of the picture, so I wasn't able to see Marvin either. I couldn't drive my car, which had no plates. And on the third day of a legitimate job I had finally landed in an attempt to simply survive, I was arrested on the way to work for some outstanding warrants—and landed in jail for five months!

It was now 1991. After I got out of jail, I heard through a friend that Carol was trying to contact me. So I headed back to Spokane, still in the car without plates, and managed to make it there, where I remained for the next three years, immersed in the drug and prostitution culture and economy. Ironically, I had Marvin with me now (Kathy had dropped him off to live with me during this time). Carol had two children, two girls. We played "house"—trying to achieve some semblancy of normalcy in an incredibly dark and chaotic lifestyle. Unfortunately, I had no idea what "normal" really looked like, or how to achieve it. But the desire was there.

Throughout this time, I tried to maintain a relationship with my sister and her kids. I would visit her when I could, at her home in the Beacon Hill neighborhood in Seattle. I also kept in touch with my adopted father. Pops had a "girlfriend" (at nearly 80 years old). He had seen all three of his wives die during his lifetime. One of his two children from his first wife was murdered at a nightclub. He had lived a difficult life.

I returned to Seattle with Marvin Jr. in January of 1994, still heavily using drugs. I sought out my adopted father, as I wanted him to know his grandson. After awhile, Carol and her two daughters joined me, and she got a real job. I, too, got some real jobs as a day laborer, and started to help my father around his place, as I had done when I was a boy.

As it turned into the summer of '94, I helped Pops with his farming of the two vacant lots adjacent to his property. He raised cucumbers, cabbage, onions, beans, and other vegetables and fruit on those lots. He made some fine wine, too. One summer I helped him make over 40 gallons of wine that he kept downstairs. Some real seeds of normalcy were planted again in my heart and life during this time, and I longed to see them grow to fruition.

One day, while visiting Marion on Beacon Hill, I met a woman named Jeanett outside of her apartment. Marion's boyfriend introduced me to her. I didn't know it at the time, but I had just met God's greatest gift to me. I asked her if she wanted to smoke some crack. She agreed, but she didn't look like an addict. She had a little three-year-old boy named Jeffery. This began a pattern of moving back and forth from Beacon Hill to see Marion, with my interest more and more being in Jeanett, and then back to Kent to see Carol. Occasionally I went back to Pops' house to see him.

On one occasion, we went to visit my cousin's house, E.J. Jr., and while we were there, my Uncle E.J. showed up. This was the first time I had seen him since the terrible court scene when I confronted him about his abuse, when I was 16. I was now 39 years old. I looked at him, now an 83-year-old man. "You got me in trouble," he said abruptly as he walked out, slamming the door behind him.

A couple of weeks later, I got a call from Pops telling me that Uncle E.J. had fallen and broken his hip, and was now in the convalescent home. I decided to go and visit him; Pops and Marion came along. When I saw my uncle, an overwhelming emotion came over me. It was not anger or bitterness for his treatment of me, but rather gratitude for what good he had put into me. "Uncle E.J. you ain't going to die here. You put a lot of things in me. You put stuff in me, Uncle E.J., that I have used in my life," I told him.

My father who had also been bullied by Uncle E.J. all of his life, watched me give honor to this man in a way I had not been able to honor him before. As we walked out of the room, I put my hand on Pop's shoulder. He quickly pulled away from my hand and looked away.

When I went back two days later to see Uncle E.J., I noticed he had softened towards me. "Marvin, you just go take care of that boy. Get yourself a job and just take care of that boy of yours." He was expressing love to me the only way he knew how. He was giving me his best advice, and it was good advice. As I walked out that day, I sensed that this would be the last time I would see this man alive, and I was right. When I heard of his death, I was glad I had been able to end with him in that way. I held nothing against him. The man had done the best he could and I was able to take what he had put into my life, even though much of it had been painful.

Deeper and Darker Still

I was now commuting back and forth between Carol's place in Kent and Jeanett's on Beacon Hill (under the auspices of visiting my sister). Now Carol was also pregnant with my child; however, I was spending more and more time with Jeanett, with our crack addiction taking control. On my 40th birthday, April 25, 1995, I took Carol to the hospital to have our daughter, Lyric. I dropped her off and went to get high with Jeanett, who was also now three months pregnant with my baby.

After Lyric was born, Carol created a system that didn't depend on me to help take care of her girl. This is what many African American women have done for generations. They have learned to build a network of support that doesn't depend upon the father. As I reflect on this, I understand it is smart, common sense survival on their part. But it is also a self-perpetuating message that lowers the expectation for father involvement by telling the father he is not important. It also appeals to a base desire of not wanting to be tied down with any long-term consequences for his behavior. This is what I experienced, as so many others have before and continue to experience. This phenomenom has all but destroyed families and communities, and seriously deteriorated the African American community, as I will explain later.

As I gravitated more and more to Jeanett in the following six months, we were constantly getting high together. When she delivered our daughter, Devotion, at Harborview Hospital in Seattle, they did a drug test. They found crack cocaine in Devotion's system and determined that this was causing her to be developmentally delayed. Thirty days after Devotion's birth, the state came in and took her out of the apartment.

But that wasn't all. One day, Jeanett and I did something very foolish. I left the house and turned off the stove. Jeanett left the house right after me and, thinking she was turning off the stove, turned it back on. We left Marvin Jr., who was now seven, with his younger siblings, Jeffery and Devotion, in the house. Soon the house was filled with smoke and the fire department was called. As I came to the house and saw the truck with flashing lights, I was greeted with, "Do you know how many times we have gone on these calls and it doesn't turn out okay? This was a terrible thing you did." I argued that I was not a bad parent, but to no avail. The facts spoke for themselves. This incident was recorded by CPS as another example that Jeanett and I were not fit parents.

All this compelled Jeannettt to enter a six-month rehabilitation program called The Mom's Project. After three months of being clean and sober, she was able to have her kids with her again. I am sad to admit, however, that I didn't understand at that time what the whole recovery process was about. When Jeanett got out of treatment, the very first thing I did was invite her to get high with me. All of that sobriety, down the drain. She began to use drugs at a higher level of intensity than before she went into treatment, and started selling crack to support her using habit. We were both out of control.

Saying Good-Bye to Pops

It was February 1997 and Pops' health was failing. We celebrated his 81st birthday and he passed away two months later. I made sure he was buried in his Sunday best, as I remembered him dressing when he was a younger man. We had a big gathering at his house and Uncle E.J.'s sons right away began talking about taking possession of his house and selling it. It was shortly after that I was given a paper stating that Marion and I would get $1,000 from my father's house but if I contested this offer, I would not get anything. Even in death my father and his children were disrespected by Uncle E.J., this time through his sons. I knew it wasn't right or fair, but what could I do about it?

I had never given Pops the honor he deserved. He was a good, honest man—a hard working man who loved Marion and me, his adopted children, the best way he knew how, by working really hard. We were taken away from him when his first wife died. He never stopped loving us, as demonstrated by the way he would provide support to us whenever he could. I will never forget the kindnesses he showed to me when I didn't deserve them. I am sorry I never showed him the love and respect he deserved.

Finally Reaching the End of Myself

One night, Jeffery's dad came home with a lump sum of money for Jeanett. She and I took a car and got high, spending several nights in a hotel room with the money and leaving Jeffery and the other kids at our house with his dad. It was 1997 now, and our home was a drug-saturated, chaos-filled environment. It was getting crazier and crazier. I knew I needed to get some help, so I went and had a drug and alcohol evaluation done. They told me I needed to go to treatment for at least 21 days.

I got into my car and headed over to West Seattle, where I got on the ferry that would take me to the treatment program. On the ride across Puget Sound, a worker clowned with me as he eyed my suitcase, "Looks like you're going on a vacation. Is that the 21-day or 28-day vacation you're going on?" He knew exactly where I was going.

I got out of treatment after 30 days and found that while I was gone, CPS had come and removed Jeffery, and placed him into a foster home. Jeanett only had Devotion in her care, but CPS was actively trying to find out where she was, so they could remove her from the home as well. We tried to hide her, but I made another big mistake. I dropped off Devotion at her childcare facility and went and got high with Carol. I forgot to retrieve Devotion and the daycare called CPS, who put her into foster care.

Any semblance of success or pride had long since disappeared. It was a miserable, day-to-day desperate existence, which was the hopeless state in which I found myself that fateful December day as I watched a CPS worker drive my seventh child away from me.

During the past four years, I had lived from chemical high to chemical high, moving back and forth from Carol's to Jeanett's house. In January of 1998, the authorities told me I had to go back into treatment if I were to ever have any chance of getting Marvette back from the state. Jeanett was completely overwhelmed by her addiction and unable to parent, but I knew deep down that I wanted to be the one to parent my children. I felt a deep remorse for reintroducing Jeanett to crack, as her addiction had now come back with a vengeance.

As April came, I began to make calls to the treatment center and I finally got the "bed date" (an opening), which was April 16th. In treatment, I slowed down enough to begin to think about my life as a whole. I was 43 years old and had never known who I really was. For 33 of those years, I had been on a futile search to belong to some kind of family. I spent much of my life without a mother or father's love and now I had seven kids from five different women—all of them growing up without my presence.

It was arranged by CPS for Marvette, who had just turned one, to visit me every two weeks for an hour while I was in treatment. That short, bi-weekly visit did so much for me to motivate me to work hard towards sobriety. It also was noticed by the other residents that I was working hard on being a committed father. It seemed to infuse hope into them, as well.

With Jeanett still in her addiction, I was preparing myself for the very real possibility that I may need to be a single father. A voice inside kept telling me I had to get Jeanett to treatment. I felt my kids would say, "Daddy you got right, but what about Mommy? What's going to happen to her?" That voice kept nagging me. But for now, if my children would have only one active parent in their life, it was likely going to be me.

At the same time, I began to realize that my misguided sexual pursuits all of these years had come from something deeper than mere sex drive. I longed to be mothered. Sex had been like a bandaid for this deeper need. I also realized that the past several years I had been under a tremendous amount of self-deception due to my drug addiction—self-deception that I had been a good father to my kids, when so much of the time I was with them I had been under the influence of crack.

The more I gathered my wits about me as the effects of my drug addiction faded, the more this realization levelled me emotionally. For so long, my addiction to crack had enabled me to escape the despair I felt deep in my heart. Where could I go now with this shame, now that I couldn't mask it anymore with drugs?

CHAPTER SIX
The Road to Recovery

Treatment was a place of tremendous healing for me, on a number of levels. While I was in recovery, almost every day seemed the same (classes, work duties, one-on-one counseling sessions, repeat.) Each day blended into the next, but I was determined to remain in the program for the sake of my children.

One day, in one of my classes, the counselor asked me, "What do you want to do with your life?"

I didn't even have to think about it and quickly answered, "I want to be a cook." It seemed logical. I worked in the kitchen at the recovery center and I was thinking about making an honest living now.

The counselor looked at me, puzzled, and said, "Why would you waste your good talent on food?" His comment had a strong impact on me. I knew I could lead others down the wrong path, but the thought had never occurred to me that my leadership abilities and people skills could be actually used to benefit others in a positive way.

At the 45-day mark, I was sober for the first time in years. But I continued to be haunted about one thing. I knew I was sober but I wasn't truly clean. I felt dirty inside. Guilt and shame were constantly staring me in the face and I had no drugs to numb the pain. I felt such remorse for the selfish decisions I had made, the women I had hurt, and more than anything, the chaos and confusion I had caused for my innocent children. What could make me clean inside?

Almost two years previously, I had dabbled with Christianity and even was baptized, but I quickly fell away from the faith when I resented church members for "not caring enough about me." Besides, Jeanett seemed relieved when I finally was done with that religious distraction so we could continue to get high together.

There were Christian services at the treatment center every Sunday, led by a pastor who was a former pimp. That caught my attention. Each Sunday for three weeks I intended to go to the service, but each Sunday I stood outside and couldn't muster up the courage to go inside. On the fourth Sunday I finally got the strength to open the door and walked in, finding a spot in the very back row. I listened to the message and watched the altar call, where folks walked to the front and gave their lives to Christ. I knew this was what I needed in order to truly change my life. The following Sunday I could hardly wait until the message was over so I could walk up to the front. I did. Shortly afterward, the pastor asked the group if anyone wanted to be baptized. I decided I needed to do it again and renew my commitment. This time, I meant business.

There were seven of us who wanted to be baptized, and the

pastor took us out to Angle Lake near Seattle for the occasion. He donned his boots and robe, got into the water, and baptized each of us, one by one. Afterwards, as we sat on a bench drying off, a bald eagle swooped over the lake, lowered its golden talons into the water, then up and flew away. There was a young lady sitting next to me on the bench, who had just been baptized. She cried, "Did you see that? Did you see that? That eagle just took all that sin out of the water!" I was stunned. All seven of us were drug addicts. We were all trying to get clean. I for one had had years of that. But I truly believe that when I was lowered into that water in Angle Lake that day, something transformational happened. Symbolically, I died with Jesus, was buried with Him, and—out of the mess I had made of my life—was raised to live a new life. My baptism was my declaration that I was a forgiven man. My sin was removed; I was sold out for Jesus and ready for a clean start.

I feel I need to share what happened after that, otherwise I do a disservice to my reader—because after I came to Christ, all hell broke loose! I returned to Cedar Hills, where I lived in a dorm with 20 recovering addicts who pledged not to use any drugs or alcohol while living in the house. I thought things were supposed to get better, because now I "had Jesus"—but they didn't right away. It was really, really hard.

At a church service, I shared my frustration and disillusionment with a man who had been a Christian for many years. And he laughed! He said to me, "Marvin, do you remember what happened to Jesus after HE was baptized? He went into the wilderness and the devil himself show up!"[8] I got it. I was not suffering anything Jesus Himself had not endured. My resolution and spirit were strengthened and my hope was renewed.

I continued to go in for urine analyses weekly to check for

any drugs in my system and was receiving a little bit of money from the state. I was now 43 years old and had never really held a legitimate job, except for those brief stints as a day laborer in the late stages of my crack addiction. When the employment agency offered me an opening at a Goodwill station in Kirkland, Washington, I took the job.

Jeanett

I was beginning to recognize that still, small voice of the Holy Spirit speaking to me when I was alone and had quieted myself from distractions. The Bible says we will be able to truly hear from God when we love Him and belong to Him.[9]

I couldn't figure out why Jeanett wasn't getting it right. But then one day, in the shower, I heard God say to me, "I can't do anything for Jeanett because you won't get out of the way." I sensed Him saying that, as a human being, I wanted to be able to say that I was the one who was helping her get clean, beause I was the one who had gotten her hooked. But God wanted to do it. He wanted the credit. And He wanted me to get out of the way. I listened. As hard as it was, I stayed away from Jeanett for a whole week. It was painful!

Then God spoke to me again, "What you feel is pain. You've never felt pain before beause you've always been high or loaded. But I'm here to tell you that I am here with you, so the pain won't be as painful." And, for the first time in my life, I learned that was exactly right. As the days went on, it didn't hurt as much. I learned in that experience how to go through the pain because God was with me in it.

I also learned that God doesn't need me to accomplish His purposes. He gives me the privilege to partner with Him, but He does the work. I am only His hands and feet. That's why I was able to hear that Voice when He said, "I want you to go to Jeanett's house and see if she needs something to eat."

I dutifully went to her apartment and knocked. As the door opened, I looked inside her dark, empty apartment. She hardly muttered any words when she wrapped her arms around me and seemed to collapse into my body. She had no food in the apartment. Her phone, lights, and heat had all been turned off. She was thinner than I had ever seen her. On her back balcony I saw she had a Hibachi grill, and was using it in a pathetic attempt to cook a frozen whole chicken. I returned with some food and left with a deep sadness and guilt in my heart. Again, I heard a voice in my spirit, but it was a much different voice than that peaceful voice of God. Instead, it was an evil voice that said to me, "Why don't you just drink that cleaning fluid and end it all?" I knew it was a demonic voice and not the voice of the Lord, and told it to leave, in Jesus' name.

God was obviously on the move because, a short time later, Jeanett entered treatment. Occasionally we were allowed to meet and discuss custody matters. During one of our meetings, a case worker pulled me aside and said to me, "She (Jeanett) has no opportunity to get your kids back and your own chances are slim to none. However, if you were married, that would be a different matter."

I wrongly interpreted this case worker's words and assumed that she was advising that we get married (to each other) in order to get our children out of the foster care system. So, that very day, while she was still in treatment, I asked Jeanett to marry me. She said, "Yes."

I took this event very seriously, reading about marriage in

my Bible every single day and praying to God, pleading that He would help make me a good husband. Pastor Donald Tatum, the man who baptized me when I was in rehab, blessed us by sponsoring our wedding. He gave us $150, rented me a tux, and Jeanett's counselor bought her a white wedding dress. God was making a way!

Jeanett and I had nothing material between us except for our children. On a pass home, we moved everything out of her apartment to close that chapter of our lives. We weren't looking back because we had nothing to look back to! We were determined to build a new life for ourselves, even if it meant starting with nothing.

New Life, New Perspective
Jeanett and I now had a job to do together, to raise our two girls, Devotion and Marvette. Besides that, I would help her raise her son, Jeffery, and she would help me raise my son, Marvin Jr. Lyric was with her mother in West Seattle. She would not live with us, but I would make sure I visited her regularly. I also had Nick in Salinas, California and Dontay in Seaside, California.

The consequences of my choices and the people I had hurt completely overwhelmed me. Besides the countless women I had hurt in the Game, I had especially hurt the mothers of these precious children. Now I wanted to be a responsible man and a faithful father. I didn't know how to do it, other than do it one step at a time, with God showing me the way.

Now that God was the Lord of my life, I no longer needed to try and aimlessly lead myself. I had Him to look up to, Him to trust in. And that's what I did as I began to navigate life with a wife and seven children, sober and completely depending on Jesus.

Raising Our Family

After Jeanett and I got married, she was still finishing up her recovery program and had to live in the specific clean and sober housing to which she had been assigned. What a unique situation we were in, a newlywed couple who couldn't even live in the same house! We were allowed weekly, supervised, one-hour visits with our kids. What agony it caused me, not being able to wrap them in my arms and tell them exactly when we would all be able to live together as a family.

"I miss you, Daddy," the girls would each say to me. My heart felt heavy and saddened after their visits, but it made me want to fight harder, work harder. I knew that God was going to reconcile this situation and we would all live together as a family; I just needed to trust in His timing. I also knew that the state of Washington was looking for longevity and comittment from us, the parents, before they placed the children back into our care.

Around Chistmas time, our pastor agreed to help us out with a loan for first and last month's rent so Jeanett and I could rent a house. Jeanett found an ad in the paper for a house in south Seattle, and we went to check it out. When we drove down the street, I instantly felt sick to my stomach. I sensed this was a place where drugs were sold and used. It looked shady. I didn't want to live in a neighborhood that would cause me to relapse. My heart longed for a peaceful, family-centered neighborhood. As we pulled into the driveway, I noticed fresh putty on the front window, indicating that the window had probably been broken by the police in a drug raid. Once we were inside of the house, I saw the electrical sockets were loose, a sign that drugs had been hidden there and probably found in the raid. "Jeanett, I don't like the feeling here. I know this was a drug house. I feel very uncomfortable. This isn't our home," I said.

However, Jeanett wasn't fazed one bit by what she saw. Where I saw a "former drug house," she could see a "future family house." She saw the master bedroom with a large bathroom and two other bedrooms. She could see the large kitchen and backyard patio where the kids could play. The driveway would allow us to have a car (when we could buy a car) parked in it, instead of on the street. She looked at me with those big brown eyes and said, "Marvin, please. Let's just do this."

The landlord told us she needed a deposit of $500 in order for us to move in, and the church generously provided us a loan for that amount. We were able to move in on Friday, January 1st, but we weren't able to get our heat and electricity turned on until Monday. The winter of 1998-1999 was one of the coldest on record so I went down to Safeway and bought about twenty-five dollars worth of logs. We burned them in our fireplace all weekend, huddling together in front of the fire to keep warm.

After some time passed, we realized life was getting very difficult without our own car. We had UA (urine analysis) appointments to go to, parenting meetings, case worker appointments, and work. Jeanett and I had both secured good, steady jobs, and I was able to purchase an '81 Crown Victoria for $700. This was the first time I had ever purchased a car with honest money I hadn't earned illegally! What a wonderful feeling that was.

God Works in Mysterious Ways

Our life was packed with meetings during this time. I chaired our Monday night AA (Alcoholics Anonymous) meetings. Thursday night was "Family Night" at the Atlantic Street Center. I led a men's group and Jeanett attended a women's group. As we were attending meetings, working our jobs, and staying sober in preparation for our children to come home, we received an incredible encouragement from the Seattle Family Center on Beacon Hill. In recognition of the dramatic progress we'd made, a lady wrote a letter of recommendation for our family, the Marvin and Jeanett Charles family, to be honored with the award of the Atlantic Street Center's "Family of the Year." This was remarkable, since our children were not even back in our home yet!

Jeanett and I dressed up for the evening. Mayor Norm Rice, Seattle's first African American mayor, and other dignitaries handed the award to Jeanett and me. I thought to myself, *Fourteen months ago I was a crack head. Only God could do this!* It made me think of Jesus' first recorded miracle, when He turned the water into wine at the wedding in Cana. I was just like that water He had turned into wine. The fact that Jeanett and I would receive a reward while we were very much still in process impacted my philosophy about awards and how they should be best used to help people make positive changes. People should be recognized and affirmed while they are still in the midst of the battle, not only after they have "made it." This is when we all need encouragement the most!

Because of this award, I was interviewed by the *Seattle Times* and a local television station ran a story about Jeanett and me. I began to see that there was a tremendous desire for people in our community to hear good news stories of ordinary people overcoming obstacles to better their lives. Our story became the main building block for what would eventually become our ministry, D.A.D.S., to tell real life stories of transformation. We were onto something that was bigger than us.

After six months of living in our new house, still with no

children, we finally had the chance to bring the kids into our home for a visit. As Jeanett and I were getting ready to pick them up, the phone rang. Even though I was just stepping out of the shower, I picked up the phone.

"Hello, is this Marvin Charles?"

"Yes," I responded, thinking this was a telemarketer.

"Mr. Charles, is your birthday April 25th, 1955?" the caller asked.

What kind of telemarketer was this? "Yes," I answered, curious now as I continued to dry off from my shower.

"Mr. Charles, my name is Karen King and I was paid by your mother, Doris Brooks, to find you. You are her firstborn child," she stated calmly.

I sat down on the sofa, trying to take this all in and fighting fiercely to hold back tears. I had been searching for my birth mother for years. Every time I attempted to find her, I came against a dead end. Now she had found me, with just a simple phone call? I couldn't help but be awestruck by the timing of when this happened—not when I was pimping or in my crack addiction. My mother found me after I had become a follower of Jesus, clean and sober, and on the very evening when my wife and I would be able to take our three children back into our home. Was it a coincidence that all of this was happening on this one particular night? I knew better.

Living as a Family

Jeanett pulled into our the driveway with Jeffery, Devotion, and Marvette. As she walked into the house, I gave them all hugs and then I pulled Jeanett aside. "Jeanett, you won't believe this. A lady called me representing my mother. My mom—my real mom—wants to meet me. This lady has some paperwork. She lives in Renton. We can go there now and I could be seeing my mom *tonight.*" I was elated and didn't want to wait another minute. "Get the kids back in the car," I announced to Jeanett without any preparation.

Now, it was her turn to sit down and take it all in. "God be doin' some ridiculous stuff," she said. We piled back into the car with the kids and headed to Karen King's house in Renton. After signing some paperwork, Mrs. King gave me the address of my mother, Mrs. Doris Brooks. She lived only 10 blocks from where we currently lived in our new home in south Seattle!

When my mother opened the door, I gave her a hug and clung to her. "I've been waiting on this hug my whole life," I blurted out. With that, I could feel her sob with joy.

"Let me look at you," she said to me. She took off my glasses so she could get a good look. Her eyes were wet with tears and we were both shaking with nervous excitement.

"Mom, let me introduce you to your grandchildren," I said to her with pride. "This is Jeffery, Devotion, and Marvette." She started to cry again and gave them each a big hug.

As it was getting darker, we decided we needed to get the kids to bed and resume our reunion the next day. When we got home and the children were in bed, Jeanett and I sat back on the couch, reflecting on the miracle that had just happened. A reunion with my children and my birth mother on the very same day! I led us in prayer: "Lord, I prayed You would put my family back together but I never would have dreamed You would do this!"

The next day was full of more surprises. We sat down at my mother's house and began looking at photo albums. Suddenly, my eyes focused on a person. "Who is this?" I knew this guy! His name was Larron and I had played Little League baseball and junior football with him.

"Oh, that's your Uncle Larron," my mother said casually.

"*Uncle* Larron? What?"

My mother explained to me that her mother was already pregnant with Larron when she became pregnant as a 14-year-old girl. The state would not allow two women in the home to be receiving government assistance so when I was born, CPS (Child Protective Services) came and removed me from the home and placed me into foster care.

I wanted to show my mother where I lived, so we got into the car and drove the few blocks to our home. As we pulled up to the house my mother took a deep breath. "You don't live *here*, do you?" Puzzled at her response, I told her

I did.

"Your uncle used to live here. This was my brother's house. We had barbeques and family gatherings here. I know this home very well." Would these surprises ever end? Turns out, there was even more to come!

The Story Spreads

Another "coincidence" occurred when my extended family of about 200 people chose that very summer to make Seattle the site for its family reunion. They move the reunion site around the country so it's in a different location every year. This particular year, Seatttle just happened to be chosen and I was able to attend and meet about 200 relatives. What an incredible feeling that was, to know that I was in fact a part of a large, loving family, when all this time I thought I had nobody.

Struck by the dramatic nature of our story, Karen King alerted the news media that a mother and her son had been reunited after 43 years. *The Seattle Times* and KING 5 News came out and ran a story. I also did a couple of local radio interviews and morning talk shows.

Soon, my mother and I were contacted by a German television network that was doing stories on great things that have happened in the 20th century. They flew us all the way to Cologne, Germany to do a live broadcast and paid us $5,000 apiece to be on the show. What an amazing experience—all of course, God's handiwork.

The day after we did the show, my mom and I were able to do some touring around Cologne. We came to a beautiful church building with an extravagant courtyard. When I saw it, all I could do was drop to my knees with tears of joy and thanksgiving, and thank God for what He had done in my life.

More Progress

By the winter of 1999, it was time for Jeanett and me to return to court to see if we could get our kids back permanently without any more involvement with the state. I felt we had jumped through every possible hoop and there wasn't much more we could do to prove ourselves. When we arrived, my expectation was that the judge would recognize our hard work and close our case. However, these were the words we heard instead: "I think I'm going to keep this case open for another six months. I will allow the children to be in the home full time now, but I will still require the Charles family to be monitored twice weekly with visits from a case worker."

This felt like a kick in my stomach. I was visibly angry. Just then a female attorney put her hand on my shoulder and said, "Mr. Charles, don't blow this now. You're almost done. I've been watching this case a long time. This will only be six months. You can do this." Her words were what I needed right on time. She was God's angel that afternoon.

During the summer of 2000, my mom flew down to Oakland to visit my biological father. When she returned she called me with some pretty crazy news. "Your dad asked me to marry him and I said yes!" This story was getting even crazier! *God was truly doin' some ridiculous stuff*, in the words of Jeanett! I couldn't believe the incredible reconciliation that God was bringing to this family. Just a couple years ago we were all scattered about, hardly even knowing the others existed.

Karen King got wind of this latest development and contacted local media outlets and our story hit the local papers and television stations once again. By now, national television networks started to pay attention. We first were contacted by a cable television show called *Beyond Chance,* which was hosted by singer Melissa Etheridge. Then ABC, NBC, and CBS all contacted us. NBC called me first, offering to fly us out for a day to be on with Bryant Gumbel. But ABC had a better offer: they would fly Mom, Dad, Jeanett, and me out to New York to be on *Good Morning America* with Diane Sawyer. On top of that, they would give us a couple of extra nights in a hotel and the resources to enjoy the sights of New York. We agreed to the show and we had the experience of a lifetime.

When we came home to Seattle, our life began to settle into a new normal. Finally, the day came when our case was closed. There was no more monitoring from CPS, no more UA tests required, no more court appearances needed. We were finally riding our family bike without training wheels and it felt really, really good. At this time my son Marvin Jr., who lived with his maternal grandparents down in the Bay area, came up to visit. I invited him to stay with us and live with us in Seattle permanently. Now we had two girls, Devotion and Marvette, and two boys, Jeffery and Marvin Jr., in our home. The only child of mine in Seattle who wasn't under our roof was my daughter, Lyric, who still lived with her mother.

The Birth of D.A.D.S.

I was now working for OASIS (Office Assembly & Systems Installation Services). The company set up office spaces throughout the Puget Sound, particularly for Microsoft in Redmond, which was rapidly expanding its international headquarters, on the way to becoming the world's largest tech company. We did get paid overtime, which helped, but I was still only making about $1200 a month.

Working for OASIS was my first job where I actually gave my employer my Social Security number. That simple fact activated an avalanche of consequences for me and about $800 per month was garnished from my meager paycheck. Because my information was now "in the system," the victims of my past behaviors (like banks to whom I had written bad checks) could now receive compensation from my labor. I found reaping the seeds I had sown many years ago to be extremely painful—so painful, in fact, that at times the temptation to go back underground was almost irresistible. The greatest thing that kept me from going backward was to look at my innocent children and the pain that I had already caused them.

Although I was working 16 to18 hours a day some days, I felt a physical fatigue as well as emotional stress from the financial burden of taking care of such a large family. Also, I learned that marriage was very hard work. As two recovering addicts, Jeanett and I were learning together what a functional, loving, Christ-centered relationship looked like. I would sometimes question her when I got discouraged by how hard it was.

"Did we do this wrong? Did we make the right choice in getting married?" Thankfully, we were able to stay in our house because we were receiving government assistance from Section 8, but Jeanett soon got laid off from her job, putting even more financial pressure upon us.

To relieve the pressure a little bit, I was able to pick up speaking engagements here and there. I could just pop in a VHS tape of the *Good Morning America* or the *Beyond Chance* segment and then tell my story. I started to make it my mission to empower fathers to get straight and be there for their families.

From there, the desire began to grow within both Jeanett and me to take what we had learned so far in our journey and help others. We had overcome many obstacles to get to where we were. But we were just two ordinary people, and we knew that what we had accomplished could be reproducible. There were practical things we had learned about dealing with the courts and the various state agencies and there were also spiritual principles of faith, honesty, prayer, and partnering with others that had made all the difference. This spiritual and practical approach meant choosing God's ways for change rather than our own. We were ready to share what we'd learned.

Jeanett came up with the name that would become well known in urban Seattle as a place of hope for men desiring to become re-engaged in the lives of their children: "Divine Alternatives for Dads Services" (D.A.D.S.). Our pastor at the time showed us how to incorporate and apply for our state business license. And, as simple as that, we founded a business together! We made business cards and started meeting with people in our living room. A movement of transformation, one family at a time, had begun in Seattle.

With time, Jeanett and I were put in contact with the director of a large non-profit organization called The Northwest Fathering Forum. He helped us get a non-profit status for D.A.D.S. and he even sponsored us. He opened our eyes to the fact that we were not alone, far from it. We were part of a movement—the fatherhood movement—that was empowering men like me throughout the nation.

BECOMING DADS

Charles Family Photos

Marvin as a baby (6 months old) - 1955

Marvin (age 8) - 1963   Marvin (age 28) - 1982

Marvin's father, Willie Cheatem
(age 12) – 1955

Marvin's mother, Doris Jean
(age 14) - 1955

Marvin's parents, reunited and married,
2002.

The Charles Family, First Easter after Reunification - 2000
L-R: Marvin Jr. (10), Lyric (5), Marvette (2), Devotion (4), Jeffery (7),
Marvin, Jeanett

Marvette (4), Lyric (6), and Devotion (6)
2001

L-R: Lyric (5), Marvette (2), Devotion (4), Marvin, Jeffery (6), Jeanett, Marvin Jr. (10), Nick (14)
2000

L-R: Devotion (6, on the floor), Marvette (4), Marvin Jr. (11), Jeanett, Jeffery (8), Lyric (7), Marvin
2002

Marvin and Jeanett renew their marriage
vows in Occidental Park in Seattle - 2005

L-R: Lyric (11), Jeanett, Nick (17, in front), Marvin, Marvin Jr. (14, above left), Marvette (9), Devotion (11), Jeffery (13) - 2005

L-R: Jamie-Michelle (9 months old), Jeanette, Marvin, Marvette (11), Devotion (13), Jeffery (15) - 2007

L-R: Jamie-Michelle (7), Jeanett, Marvin, Devotion (20), Lyric (20),
Dontay (29), Marvette (18)
ALL the girls, L-R Devotion (20), Lyric (20), Jamie-Michelle (7),
Marvette (18)
Dontay (20) and Marvin
2016

Marvin and Jamie-Michelle (7)
Marvin and Jeanett
2016

CHAPTER SEVEN
The Causes and Effects of Fatherlessness

I want to take some time away from my own story to talk about the issue of fatherlessness in America, because my story is just a microcosm of what is happening on a national level in exponential proportions. Bear with me while I hit you with some facts and statistics. It's important to understand how my life fits into this larger context.

As an urban young man of color growing up in the 1980s, my life—like so many others—was "set up" to perpetuate fatherlessness. A young man like me generally didn't know his father and saw a mother trying to provide for him by working long hours, yet still needing government assistance. In the media, he saw dramatic images of African American athletes and entertainers hitting the jackpot, receiving respect and admiration. The hip hop culture and rap music glorified the drug culture of the street as a way to provide the lifestyle he dreamed of having.

Popularized by movies like *Super Fly* and *Mack*, drugs became instinctively fashionable in urban America for those who were involved in the fast life. Drug dealers moved into and took over "the projects" (housing developments) and, being the opportunists they were, waited for the mothers on welfare to get their checks. The men who often lived with these women used and sold drugs until they went to prison, died, or moved on to another woman.

In the early '60s and '70s, cocaine in particular was a drug that only people of means could access. This drug came in powder form. However, in the late '70s, "freebasing" was introduced. This is a method in which the cocaine is liquefied, dried, and scraped into a much more potent powder form that can then be smoked. By the '80s, a much cheaper process came along to manufacture this drug, which came to be known as "crack."

By the '90s, crack infiltrated the heart of America's inner cities by way of gangs and another movie, *Scarface*, which set the stage for how gangs and violence would become a norm in America. Selling cocaine became a way for many young urban men to make money in the 1980s. As more and more young men got into this competition, territories were established and gang activity and violence increased. It was a tumultuous time. This is when racial profiling began to become common practice by police departments. Often a police officer would pull over a carload of African American kids and they would have Uzi machine guns in the car with them.

These kids all came from single parent homes without a father present, as their fathers were by this time often in prison. The American criminal justice system tried to deal with the illegal selling of drugs in the urban core the best it could. The solution they came up with to curb the violence and get the drug sellers off of the street was incarceration. During the 1980s, an African American man could get 25 years for selling a hundred dollars of cocaine (two grams). It was common for a white man during that time to receive six months probation for the same crime. In 1992, there were more black men in prison than in college.[10] This, along with the racial profiling, fueled anger in the African American community and, unfortunately, a sense of justification for the illegal activity in which we were involved.

As the 1980s turned into the '90s, the culture of drugs and violence among fatherless young men of color continued. The violence and drive by shootings increased, and an "I don't care" mechanism seemed to kick into overdrive. More and more of our young people were killed through the violence. In people's minds, they were dying just trying to take care of their mamas, to give them a better life. The lure of easy money and a taste of the good life were too much for fatherless, directionless young men to resist.

"For the best part of thirty years
we have been conducting a vast experiment with the family,
and now the results are in: the decline of the two-parent,
married-couple family has resulted in poverty, ill-health,
educational failure, unhappiness, anti-social behavior,
isolation and social exclusion for thousands of women,
men and children."

—Rebecca O'Neill, Experiments in Living: *The Fatherless Family*

Roots of Fatherlessness

In the 1940s and '50s in the Central District of Seattle where I grew up, an area of about four square miles, the majority of the population was predominantly mixed race. They were hard working people who taught their children to be "seen and not heard." In that kind of environment, Dad and Mom worked so their children could get an education and a better life. There was a structure to the family and a rhythm to life.

However, there was not a lot of emotional connection from parents to children; the generation gap was a real thing. When parents told children to "do as they were told," it was largely out of fear. With Jim Crow laws still in place in many places around the country, black parents knew that any misbehehavior in their children could have serious and painful repercussions. When crises occurred in families—like divorce or a death—they were not explained to children. Kids were not generally able to turn to their parents for understanding, healing, or guidance. They—and I can safely say "we"—turned to our peers to help us figure out how to navigate life.

Alcohol was usually a big part of the home life in my community. After working so many hours, there was a sense of being entitled to it, to use it to relax. Our fathers would "let their hair down" on the weekends especially—gambling, going to the taverns, and in Seattle the jazz cabarets and underground music scene. A mother with her children didn't get to do that. As fathers engaged in this lifestyle, they often met other women and would abandon their homes. Sometimes they would impregnate those women and then abandon them. This is one of the roots of what is happening today in our communities.

When the 1960s came, the "do as you're told" mentality

didn't work anymore with African American youth. Tensions erupted. With the Civil Rights movement and the breakdown of traditional marriage in American culture as a whole, more and more urban children were born out of wedlock and were raised by single moms and grandmothers. The ensuing riots after Martin Luther King, Jr. was assassinated brought the tension to a boiling point in many urban neighborhoods, causing a "white flight." This all set the stage for the 1970s and 1980s, when drugs flooded into urban America.

The 1970s was a period of much uncertainty in the American economy as a whole. We can all remember the gas lines, high unemployment, and inflation. This hit urban areas especially hard. An underground economy started to develop where many men looked at illegal activity as necessary to survive and take care of themselves. My life as a pimp began during those years, though I am not proud of it now. It seemed to me, and others like me, a legitimate lifestyle choice at the time, given the options as I saw them.

Generational Patterns

In my work at D.A.D.S., I often speak to men about my beginnings, with a 14-year old mother and a 20-year old father, born out of wedlock. I ask them, "How many of you would allow your 14-year old daughter to go out with a 20-year old man?"

They almost universally and unanimously answer,

"No way!"

Then I come back to them with, "How can you stop it if you're not there?"

Teen pregnancies, out of wedlock births, and single mother homes are just a few of the many negative results of fatherlessness. The chances of a child growing up in poverty just because of that one fact alone are greatly increased; in fact, children in fatherless homes are almost four times more likely to be poor. In 2011, 12% of children in married-couple families were living in poverty, compared to 44% of children in mother-only families.[12]

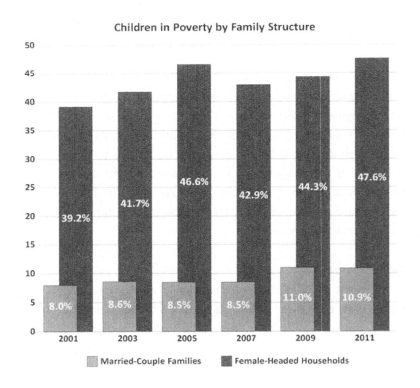

Children in Poverty by Family Structure

Besides poverty and out of wedlock pregnancy, consider the other documented "fruits" of the fatherlessness epidemic:

1. Drug and Alcohol Abuse

Children in single parent homes are substantially at risk for alcohol abuse.[14] Additionally, the U.S. Department of Health and Human Services states, "Fatherless children are at a dramatically greater risk of drug and alcohol abuse."[15]

2. Diminished Physical and Emotional Health

In a study of 1,977 children aged three and older who were living with a residential father or father figure, it was found that children living with married biological parents had significantly fewer behavioral problems (both externalizing and internalizing) than children living with at least one non-biological parent.[16] Tragically, children of single-parent homes are more than twice as likely to commit suicide.[17]

3. Lower Educational Achievement

It has been well-documented that children living with their married biological father test at a significantly higher level than those living with no or a non-biological father. And, children in grades seven to12 who have experienced divorce, separation, or out of wedlock birth had lower grade point averages than those who had always lived with both biological parents.[18] Along the same lines as these findings, 71% of high school dropouts are fatherless; fatherless children have more trouble academically, scoring poorly on tests of reading, mathematics, and thinking skills. Children from father-absent homes are more likely to be truant from school, more likely to be excluded from school, more likely to leave school at age 16, and less likely to attain academic and professional qualifications in adulthood.[19]

4. Involvement in Crime

Compared to peers in intact families, adolescents in single-parent families and stepfamilies are more likely to engage in delinquency.[20] A study using data from the National Longitudinal Study of Adolescent Health explored the relationship between family structure and risk of violent acts in neighborhoods. The results revealed that if the number of fathers is low in a neighborhood, there is an increase in acts of teen violence. The statistical data showed that a 1% increase in the proportion of single-parent families in a neighborhood is associated with a 3% increase in an adolescent's level of violence.[21] Children age 10 to 17 living with two biological or adoptive parents were significantly less likely to experience sexual assault, child maltreatment, other types of major violence, and non-victimization types of adversity. They were also less likely to witness violence in their families compared to peers living in single-parent families and stepfamilies.[22]

5. Sexual Activity and Teen Pregnancy

Teens in fatherless homes are far more likely to be sexually active than adolescents living with their fathers.[23] As a result, teen pregnancy rates are higher, as well. Being raised by a single mother raises the risk of teen pregnancy, marrying with less than a high school degree, and forming a marriage where both partners have not finished high school—virtually guaranteeing a self-perpetuating cycle.[24]

I have seen the pain of fatherless daughters up close and personally. When I was still in the fast life, during the 1990s, I met a woman with two daughters. I did not father these girls. I tried to be a father figure of some kind to them, even though

I was still caught up with my cocaine addiction. Recently I met these two women again. One was 39 years old and the other 29. The older woman had three children from different fathers and the younger one had five children from five different men. The younger one said to me, "I finally caught up to my dad and he wants nothin' to do with me. I guess you're supposed to be my dad." Though it was quite an honor that she would say that to me, it still breaks my heart.

My daughter Marvette has friends at school who, sadly, refer to their biological fathers as "my sperm donor." Fatherlessness has been extremely destructive to the self-esteem of African American women, as well as to men. It is self-perpetuating now. This curse, I believe, can only be reversed one man and one family at a time.

Sadly, the ultimate assurance of father absence (besides death) is prison. Among many African American men, going to prison has become just like the fast life; gangs have been glorified in the "hood" and to be in one is considered "cool." The father in prison, strange as it may sound, has almost become idolized and glorified. It doesn't seem to dawn on folks about the waste and tragedy of it until they begin to see three generations incarcerated. That's right, grandfather, son, and grandson all in prison at the same time!

> *"For boys, the most socially acute manifestation*
> *of paternal disinvestment is juvenile violence.*
>
> *For girls, it is juvenile and out-of-wedlock childbearing.*
>
> *One primary result of growing fatherlessness*
> *is more boys with guns.*
>
> *Another is more girls with babies."*
>
> —David Blankenhorn, *Fatherless America*

A Picture of Fatherlessness

Fatherlessness goes beyond the boundaries of race, culture, and socio-economic status. It has tremendous effects on our culture at large, exponentially so as it plays out in the life of a child. It makes a huge difference in the development of his or her identity. It renders him/her highly susceptible to negative peer influence, and to making poor life decisions—including drugs, out of wedlock pregnancies, and criminal behaviors.

Children who go down these life paths often do so in an ill-fated attempt to fill the void left in them by their absent fathers. They seek love, comfort, and security, but do so inappropriately, ending up with more children like themselves conceived not out of love, but out of a need to be loved. As ill-equipped parents, they try to raise these children without a job or money, many of them continuing their drug habits and leaving the children in a state of dire need, if not outright abandoning them. These children will likely not have both parents involved in their lives. So, without any real, lasting intervention, the cycle continues and expands—unless an individual does what it takes to stop it.

Take Walt, for example (not his real name, although he is a real person and a client at D.A.D.S.). Walt is an African American man who was raised by his mother and sisters. He occasionally connected with his father, especially as he played sports in his teen years. But as he grew older, Walt lost interest in sports. His mother worked long hours and he had a great deal of unsupervised time. He gravitated to the streets, his peers, and eventually to criminal behavior. They held an attraction his home didn't have. In his eyes, he was becoming a "man" by increasingly taking chances, moving away from his mother's influence, gaining acceptance from his friends, and having money in his pocket.

Walt was living out a street drama that happens all the time to young men who are raised by single mothers. This is how it goes: Imagine a boy, about 13 years old, being raised by his mother. She asks him to get her a glass of water from the kitchen as she kicks off her shoes after a long day at work. He obediently responds to her as he has done his entire life.

One day he goes outside to play basketball with some neighbor boys. "Hey, look at the mama's boy. You wanna play? Okay, come on," the biggest kid says to him. He sheepishly steps onto the court and begins to play. Before too long, he goes up for a rebound and takes an elbow on the chin. He begins to cry.

"Why don't you go home, mama's boy, if you can't play with the big boys?" He walks home dejectedly, head down.

"What's wrong, son?" his mother asks when he walks in the door.

"Nothin'," the boy responds.

The next time his mother asks him to get her something from the kitchen, his response is, "I don't feel like it." He has changed. She is puzzled and sighs, and gets up to fetch her own glass of water.

A while later, the boy goes back to the basketball court and is allowed to play. This time, when he takes an elbow to the face, he throws an elbow back. "Hey, kid, you're all right. You can play with us anytime," the biggest kid says casually after the game.

Trying to act cool, the younger boy responds suavely, "Cool. See ya later." He goes home and is strengthened in his new sense of manhood that is bolstered by his defiance of his mother. He has no father to sit him down and say, "Don't you disrespect your mama or you'll answer to me; you understand, boy?" Of course, the mother can advocate for herself; but especially when it comes to keeping an adolescent boy in check, there comes a time when size matters!

Walt, like so many others who share a similar story, eventually took to the streets and a lifestyle of crime. At 25, he was caught and sent to prison, and was released two years later. By this time, he had fathered four children by two different mothers, and was now being held responsible for them by the state. In his heart of hearts, he wanted to do things the right way and be a responsible, committed father. But Walt worked a low-paying job and almost all of his money was gobbled up by child support. What could he do? Out of frustration, he returned to what he knew— the criminal lifestyle, selling drugs. Again, he was caught and sent to prison, this time for 14 years.

When Walt received an early release after his second term in prison, he came to D.A.D.S., now owing a whopping $133,000 in back child support. Hopeless and feeling helpless and defeated, Walt lamented, "I'm paying for a house I will never live in."

Perseverance Pays Off

It is hard to explain to those who have not walked in the shoes of the men who walk through my door at D.A.D.S. in Seattle, but let me try. Let's say a man is coming out of prison and wants to "do the right thing," to be a responsible father to his children. He has had it with prison. He doesn't want to go back. He wants to become involved in the lives of his children. He longs to help provide for them and their future as he works a job and rebuilds his life.

These are noble desires but there are many obstacles that prevent him from succeeding. First of all, if he has a criminal record, it is very difficult for him to find a job. If he is able to secure a legitimate job, where he provides a Social Security number, soon all of the thousands of dollars that have been accumulating in his arrearage account hit him like a ton of bricks. He is often labeled as "abusive" by the mother or mothers of his children, which can keep him from access, or strongly limit access, to supervised visits. He is "guilty until proven innocent" in the family court system. The lure of returning to drug or alcohol addiction or criminal behavior is very strong as he hits these walls and goes back into his old environment of friends and family. But at D.A.D.S., we have found it doesn't have to end there.

I want to circle back to Walt. When Walt came to D.A.D.S., shortly after being released from prison for the second time, two of his children were living near Portland, a three-hour drive from where Walt was living in Seattle. We were able to help him modify his child support payment down to $11,000, which he could reasonably pay off. He began driving back and forth to Portland twice a month, picking up his children and then returning them, so they would have their father's influence in their life on a regular basis. He eventually married a wonderful woman who was supportive of his role as a non-custodial father and began to build a stable, lasting marriage and home environment.

Walt stayed connected to all five of his children, giving them encouragement and input as they moved through their pre-teen and teen years. He also stayed connected to the D.A.D.S. community, and even worked for D.A.D.S. helping other men turn their lives around. As of this writing, each of his five children has either graduated from college or is currently attending college. None of them have fallen into criminal behavior as their father did.

Walt's story is not unusual at D.A.D.S.; that is the transformation from generational fatherlessness to committed fatherhood we see time and time again. What are the keys to Walt's turn around that have changed the destiny of his children and probably his grandchildren? What is the secret to the countless other "Walts" who have changed the course of their lives and families at D.A.D.S.? It really isn't rocket science. In fact, it's what the next chapter is all about.

CHAPTER EIGHT
Reversing the Curse

A sign hangs prominently in our D.A.D.S. office: "And He will turn the hearts of the fathers to their children and the hearts of the children to their fathers, or else I will smite the land with a curse" (Malachi 4:6). This last verse in the Old Testament speaks of the very real "curse" of fatherlessness that we are seeing in our nation. We can see what the effect of this curse looks like, as well as the consequences it has on children, mothers, familial units, and society at large. But is there a way to stop it?

I believe there is, but it isn't just a question of changing policy or instituting more social programs. I believe that "reversing the curse" is a matter of the human *heart* changing, starting with the father toward the child, and then the child toward the father. But before this can happen, a father's heart has to change toward himself and toward God. Most of the men we work with have never been validated. And until that happens, their hearts remain unchanged.

At D.A.D.S., we've seen men's hearts soften and turn towards their children. We've witnessed them overcoming huge obstacles in order to reconnect with their children and become involved, responsible fathers. When this happens, a generational curse of fatherlessness down family lines begins to be reversed and a beautiful legacy of fatherhood begins. We have seen this happen in countless families as well as my own.

We Need More Fatherhood Success Stories

A man named Bill came into our D.A.D.S. office one day. "I heard you can help me get me out of paying my child support," he told me bluntly. I knew he had the wrong impression of what we do, but I invited him anyway to our Bible study group that meets every Thursday night. He continued to attend, even after discovering we weren't going to help him get out of paying his child support.

After he had been attending D.A.D.S. for a while, Bill came home one day and witnessed his aunt and son—with whom he lived—fighting in front of the house. Enraged by the disrespect with which his son was treating his aunt, Bill jumped in and joined the fight. Shaken by the incident afterwards, he immediately drove over to my house. "Marvin, I'm afraid someone may have called the police. I didn't know where else to go."

My heart sank for Bill. Deep down, I was remembering having walked the same path he was on. I thought, *I've been blessed by God, to be where I am now after being where I've come from. Change is possible!* This connected us deeply and opened up a whole new level of freedom and momentum for Bill. He knew things had to change. He was starting to believe things could change. And he was recognizing that the change had to start in his own heart and life.

As we continued to walk with Bill at D.A.D.S., he began to learn how to negotiate his child support payments instead of just avoiding them. Bill was a wiz with technology and electronics, and started to rebuild his life to the place where he could support himself and his family through these skills and not through selling drugs. He began to serve at D.A.D.S. as our video and sound man when we traveled and made presentations.

On one trip, we attended a conference at Pepperdine University in Malibu, California. While we were there, Bill surprised me with some new information. "Hey Marvin, I've got a son down here in southern California." In his old life, Bill had married a woman (under an assumed name), and had abandoned her and the baby when the child was only two years old. Bill wondered if this was a good time to find and connect with his son.

After praying about it, determining the timing was right, and making some phone calls, Bill was soon in touch with the mother of his son—and was able to meet him for the first time in fourteen years. To his surprise and delight, Bill's 16-year-old son held no animosity; he just wanted to see his dad! That was just the beginning of the favor that would be poured out upon Bill as he took one step at a time to rebuild his life and reconnect with his children.

For example, one Sunday when Bill's car wouldn't start and he'd planned on going to church, he persevered and jumped on his bicycle and rode it to church instead. After the message that morning, he was standing in the foyer of the church visiting when a man in a wheelchair suddenly broke into the conversation. "Boy, I know you! I'm your uncle and your dad's been looking for you for 30 years!"

BECOMING DADS

Soon afterward, Bill was on another trip to California with me to help me with my audio video system, only this time he was the one reconnecting with his own father, in Palm Springs. In that reunion, he learned much about his biological father. Bill could now understand the reason behind his father's absence for all those years and was filled with a new perspective and understanding he didn't have before.

Step by step, Bill was cleaning up his life and gaining ground toward a healthy, happy, productive life. As he began to grow in his relationship with Christ, he became clean and sober. He discontinued an inappropriate living situation. He gave his time to help others. In fact, as part of his recovery and life transformation, Bill served the D.A.D.S. program in every way he could. Not only skilled with electronics and technology, he was also good with tools and started a very successful handyman business. Eventually Bill found a job with a large national corporation and today he holds a key IT position in their technology nerve center on the corporate campus.

Bill's story is still unfolding but there continue to be promising signs in his family. At my recommendation, he flew both his son and daughter from California to Seattle for a visit, where, through his connections at work, he was able to find jobs for them, as well. With their income, they are now able to help support their mother. This action has also allowed him to reconcile with the mother of his children. The tone of the family has changed from one of hostility and estrangement to peace and a conciliatory relationship.

Another great result of these connections is that his son is now living and working in Palm Springs, and has a warm and growing relationship with his grandfather, with whom Bill was also reunited. When Bill sees his son, they "jam" together through music, a talent that his son inherited from Bill. Three generations of fathers and sons are now in relationship and committed to building and supporting their families and being responsible citizens. These are the curse-reversing stories we're looking for.

Roots of Generational Fatherlessness

Before proposing what I think may be some tangible solutions to the fatherlessness crisis, I'd first like to recognize what causes the cycle of fatherlessness in the first place. *Why is it a cycle that persists from generation to generation?*

Research indicates that divorce and having children outside of marriage are the two largest contributors to fatherlessness. It is estimated that 33% of children in the United States are growing up in homes that are absent their biological father. That's 24.7 million children (one out of every three), up from only 224,000 in 1960.[25] The divorce rate has also increased rapidly. There are approximately 876,000 divorces every year in the United States, and it is estimated that 41% of all first marriages end in divorce. The divorce rate has doubled since 1960.[26] The devastating consequences of family deterioration cannot be overstated. Families without fathers, no matter what their ethnicity, generally occupy the bottom portion of America's economic layout.

We see this truth played out in the poverty rates, which for single parent families are five times those for married families. In 2009, 37% of single parent families were raising their children in poverty, while only 6.8% of married couples with children were poor. Fatherless families are almost four times more likely to raise their children living in poverty.[27] The numbers are simply staggering.

BECOMING DADS

The Third Way think tank reported: *"There is a great deal of evidence that children from single parent homes have worse outcomes on both academic and economic measures than children from two parent families. . . . there is a vast inequality of both financial resources and parental time and attention between one- and two-parent families."* The study report also states, " . . . *most one parent families are headed by mothers not fathers, and boys appear to do relatively worse in these families, pehaps due to paternal absence."* [28]

Back to my original question: Why does the cycle of fatherlessness persist? Well, for one, when children grow up in a single parent home, it becomes their version of "normal." Because they know no different, they will likely perpetuate the cycle by also becoming pregnant or fathering a child outside of marriage. And, since families on welfare lose 10-20% of their benefits as soon as they wed, marriage isn't too high on the priority list for single mothers.

For example, when I met Jeanett, I was going back and forth between her household and Carol's. Carol's "normal" was to work a nine to five job, as she was raised in a stable, two-parent household where her parents both worked. However, Jeanett's "normal" was to live as a single parent depending on state assistance. She had been culturally conditioned to this lifestyle.

Jeanett started using drugs at an early age, 12. When she became pregnant with Jeffery at 26 years old, she was in treatment. She carried Jeffery while clean and sober, and qualified for Section 8 Housing, which was offered to mothers who were pregnant out of wedlock. (Programs like Section 8 Housing are federally funded through block grants, but administered by the individual states.)

Rather than having one area known as "the projects," as had been common in the past, this program was "portable." Jeanett would pay a landlord, for instance, as little as $35 a month to rent an apartment, along with a voucher the landlord would send to the state to be reimbursed for the full amount of the rent. For Jeanett and countless other low-income, single mothers in the United States, the government became the "father" (provider) in her household, just as it had been when she was growing up.

There are conditions the government puts on the single mother to have this privilege. Jeanett could receive this benefit as long as no one else lived in the home with her. The landlord was responsible for policing this. However, when crack cocaine entered the picture, the process often went sideways. In some cases, the landlord and the tenant would use drugs together, until illegal activity was reported and the police had to enter the picture to stop it. In other cases, the tenants would allow their units to become bases of operations for drug dealers, with or without the landlords' knowledge. Needless to say, this system was prone to corruption on a number of levels.

The bottom line was that I would stay often with Jeanett, but always left after a day or two so as not to endanger her benefit. It is worth noting that the financial agreement she had with the state created a huge disincentive for a working, committed man to live with her permanently.

Shooting Ourselves in the Foot

As a result of this and other factors, we as a nation have a huge population of communities that are fatherless, and which are being de-incentivized by government programs and regulations from ever changing the situation. I firmly believe that—personal choices aside—fatherlessness in the low-income community in America is largely the result of the unintended negative consequences of systems that were originally designed to *help* families, but ended up having the opposite effect. Many years ago, the U.S. government set up the prototype of the current social welfare systems to provide for mothers and their children when their husbands failed to return from war. This well-intentioned attempt by the federal government to assist widows and orphans planted a seed that would contribute to a bitter harvest of fatherlessness in America generations later.

For example, my maternal grandmother was the single mother of six children by five fathers. She relied on government assistance for housing and a small stipend, supplementing her income through house cleaning. At that time, government representatives made monthly visits to make sure there was no evidence of a man in the house so she could maintain her eligibility for assistance. She would need to make sure there were no signs of wealth or luxury in the home. The television would be covered over with a blanket and put in the closet.

My mother was only 14 years old when I was born. Like many children in the urban core today, she was raised more by her peers than by a parent or parents—with no father in the home and a mother consumed with trying to provide for the family. She struggled in school, and attended an alternative high school for kids who couldn't keep up with the mainstream. After I was taken away from her by the state when I was six months old, she was haunted for many years wondering what became of me. I was plagued by not knowing who my mother and father were. This pattern that my grandmother, mother, and I experienced continues to this day in urban America . . . where seven out of 10 children are growing up without a father in the home, many not even knowing who their biological fathers *are*.

Ironically, most if not all of the studies I've seen appear to make the point abundantly clear that father absence is a major force behind many of the attention-grabbing issues that dominate the news today: crime and delinquency, premature sexuality, out-of-wedlock and teen births, deteriorating educational achievement, depression, substance abuse, alienation among teenagers, and the growing number of women and children in poverty. Are we in some ways creating the very problems we are trying to solve? It would appear so.

As I've already stated, there is much evidence that fatherlessness, criminal behavior, and incarceration all go hand in hand; research supports this fact. Study after study has shown that children, particularly boys, who grow up in fatherless homes are much more likely to fall into a delinquent lifestyle and get arrested or go to jail at some point in their lives. Why? Because they don't have a male figure in their life modeling proper behavior, respect, work ethic, and discipline. And, once a young man falls into a criminal lifestyle and ends up in prison, he is likely leaving his own children behind, causing them to live in a father-absent home just like he did. It's another aspect of the vicious and tragic cycle that we must work to halt.

In my work at D.A.D.S. today, I encounter these situations all the time. Just the other day I talked to a man who had recently been released from prison for charges ranging from theft to murder. When he came to our office, he said to me, "The only thing I've learned to do is pull a trigger." He has children with seven different mothers. Each of those mothers would likely tell of having multiple children from multiple fathers. These women are conditioned to not need or depend upon the men who impregnated them.

In fact, for a woman with children from multiple fathers, there are strong reasons to not have the fathers around, as this can cause much friction in her life, between her and the different men. It is just easier for her and the children to have the men out of their lives. So yes, men get caught up in a criminal life style, make foolish choices, and tell themselves their children are better off without them. At the same time, these single women, fueled by strong financial incentives, push them away.

What Can WE Do to Stop the Cycle?

As we examine all of the cultural and societal issues that contribute to fatherlessness, it's important to reflect on ourselves and what lies and stereotypes we, personally, have believed when it comes to poverty, crime, and father-absent homes. Have we been helping to perpetuate the issue without even knowing it? Here are three common false assumptions that come to mind:

1. "Fathers aren't needed as much as mothers. Moms are better parents."

Let's take a moment to note the impact of negative self-fulfilling prophesies. When a man hears from others (whether from parents, counselors, employers, pastors, friends, or strangers on the street) that he is no good, he will eventually begin to believe it to be true. *Oh, they say I'm worthless? Guess I must be.* The same goes for telling fathers they're not needed, or that mothers make better parents. People will begin to fulfill these words spoken over them and check out before they even get the chance. How can we expect them to succeed when they're set up for failure?

I can personally attest to the power and consequences of negative words. When I was young, the two people from whom I had wanted to feel affirmation were first my father (the man I found out later was actually my adopted father), and my Uncle Joe. I had always looked up to Joe. I have memories of him taking me hunting, fishing, and on family outings before that fateful day when my adoptive mother died.

By the time I was 18, Joe had become successful enough to move into a large, beautiful home overlooking Lake Washington. One day he said to me, "Marvin, can I talk to you for a minute?" He looked concerned.

"What's up, Uncle?" I replied.

He put his hand on my shoulder soberly. "Marvin, I don't want you to be coming around here no more. I've got teenagers in this home and you ain't a good influence on them," he told me.

I don't remember what I said in response, but what I heard in my soul was, *Marvin, you're no good. Nobody believes in you. You might as well be as bad as they think you are. You will always be guilty until proven innocent.* This was the real root of the madness I lived in from age 18 to 43, for 25 years of my life. I know I'm not alone in this, and the statistics as well as the personal testimonies I hear back me up.

2. "Once an addict, always an addict."

This mindset believes that once a parent falls into the throes of addiction, he/she should lose his or her chances to ever live with his or her children. I do understand the culture of recovery, where once a person struggles with addiction, he is labeled an addict for life. I agree that there are many, including myself, who because of their past should not touch a drop of alcohol. But when this term "addict" becomes a person's identity, I believe it goes too far. That label becomes a heavy burden for a person seeking to begin to do the right thing, to live responsibly and soberly.

One man we worked with had a past criminal record and had struggled with addiction, though was at this time in recovery. This father had three children, ages 13, seven, and four years old. One day, the grandfather called the children and one of them mentioned he was hungry. The grandfather immediately jumped to conclusions and called CPS (Child Protective Services), saying, "He's at it again." Shortly after that, the children were picked up and put into the foster care system. This was not good for the children nor the father—nor was it at all merited in this situation. It was all based on hearsay and past experience.

What is needed in these kinds of situations is a paper trail of documentation that shows that the father is making progress in such areas as supporting himself, being sober, and learning to be an effective father. If an accusation is made, this documentation could serve as a protection for the father and for the children, so that decisions are based on the current reality, not presuppositions. This is why I like to teach the men with whom we work to use the court's system of documenting everything they do, to show progress. They need to learn how to, with honesty and integrity, use the system to work for them, not against them.

3. "This is a black issue."

I'd like to clear the air right now and say that fatherlessness is not a race issue. It's a class and culture issue, spanning across all races and ethnicities. The increase in number of single-parent homes has repeatedly been painted as a problem exclusively rooted in the black community. However, that fact couldn't be further from the truth. We must acknowledge that the number of single parent homes in the United States has tripled since the 1960s, and while most of the heads of those households are black or Hispanic women, there are also many single white mothers, as well as a growing number of households led by black, single fathers. So, although data might tell us that "most black mothers are single," we cannot ignore the minority races who are in strong marriages and leading happy, healthy households, or the black dads who are stepping up as single fathers (a number that has grown every year since 2011).[29]

What Needs to Change?

In order to work toward solutions, I think we need to start a frank discussion of the changes that need to take place in American culture. Are there ways our culture, as a whole, is contributing to the problem of fatherlessness? I believe there are. For one, we spend billions of dollars treating a result, drug abuse, while we allow one of its most significant causes, father absence, to be relatively ignored.

In 2011, taxpayers spent $745 billion on federal welfare programs, compared to $400 billion in 1990.[30] Every year, the amount spent on welfare for needy families increases. This is not to say we need to do away with welfare altogether (Lord knows we relied on it when we were recovering, and without it Jeanett and I wouldn't have been able to get back on our feet), but perhaps some adjustments could be made. Are families becoming too dependent on it?

As mentioned earlier, women from impoverished families have learned throughout generations how to get by and raise a family and maintain a home without the help of a man.

It's important to recognize that a mother generally receives far more from welfare if she is single than if married. As soon as she chooses to get married and has a husband living in the home, her benefits can be cut anywhere from 10 to 20%. Then, when a couple does marry and their income nears the limits prescribed by the welfare system, a few extra dollars in income can cause thousands of dollars in benefits to be lost. What all of this means is that the two most important routes out of poverty—marriage and work—are heavily taxed under the current U.S. system.

The Aha Moment

Let's turn from macro to micro. Every one of these statistics I have quoted represents real people—a real father and mother and children. I believe the end of the cycle must begin with each of these individuals having that personal "aha" moment in his or her life where he/she says, "I'm no longer going to be one of those statistics."

I had that aha moment personally when I was 43 years old and realized that my life was not the fulfilling life I wanted, surrounded by my children. I simply was tired of doing what I had been doing, and knew that unless I changed, Jeanett and I would continue in the same vicious cycle of drug use.

When our daughter Marvette was born and I became the primary caregiver to her while Jeanett was still in the throes of addiction, this was my "aha moment." I had skin in the game. I knew that unless I changed, this precious girl, with whom I had bonded through caring for her daily needs, would be doomed to the life of fatherlessness I had experienced. For so long, I had prided myself in being a "functional addict," but when I lost Marvette, I knew unless I changed radically, I would lose her forever and she would lose me. The lie had to stop. My life was not sustainable. My coping mechanisms consisted of running from my pain, first through the fast life and later cocaine addiction. It had all caught up with me and multi-generational fatherlessness was now affecting my children. Something inside me cried, "Enough!" I knew that Marvette and my other children needed their daddy. I was now going to do all I could do to be there for them.

I'm committed to helping other fathers come to that same place of reckoning. We must break the cycle.

BECOMING DADS

CHAPTER NINE
Working within the System

There is no worse description of single fathers who have gone underground than the label of "deadbeat dad." This is a terribly unjust condemnation to put upon a man who finds himself in the no-win situation of being damned if he does (seeking legitimate work and paying what the system says he owes for child support) and damned if he doesn't (going off the radar, doing "under the table" day labor jobs, or engaging in criminal behavior).

It's not as simple as it may sound to those who are not intimately acquainted with the realities of these kinds of situations. It's important to understand that there are factors in the system that drive a father away from the mother, and away from his children, even if deep inside he wants to be responsible and have a real relationship with his child.

What these men need—the ones who truly want to be involved in their kids' lives—is not a label, more condemnation, or more penalties leveled at them. That's why, when I hear the term "deadbeat dad," it really bothers me. It can be an unfair stereotype. Most of the men I have walked alongside over the years are men who want to do the right thing. They are men who oftentimes did not have a father in their lives, but don't want the generational curse to continue. They just need the know-how and encouragement to proceed.

First: Facing Reality

One day a father came into D.A.D.S. with his 13-year old son. The boy had been with his father for a visit and the time had come for him to return to his mother. Unfortunately, the living situation at his mother's house was not a good one, and the son did not want to return; he wanted to stay with his dad.

Although this father's first response was to jump in with both feet and take his boy in right away, we had to help him take a longer-term view. He had never implemented a parenting plan and was not in a particularly great spot himself. We asked him: Where would they live? (He didn't have a permanent living arrangement.) How would he support his son? (He didn't have a steady job.) How would he be able pay the back child support he owed? (This would certainly come due when he applied for custody.) How would his current lifestyle affect or be affected by a child in his life full time?

These are the kinds of questions we help all our clients answer when they want to take on the responsibility of parenting their children. Many times the decision to parent is made emotionally, in the heat of the moment, without a clear understanding of the things that need to be put in place or the system that must be successfully navigated for that scenario to be successful.

Sometimes a reality check is in order.

With this particular father, we first helped him obtain the necessary court documents to start the process. He would need to complete the paperwork and file it with the court, serve papers to the mother, and set a court date. We advised him that, at his hearing, many things would be considered: whether this move would be in the best interest of the child, for example, and any other dynamics the judge might need to consider to make his or her determination on a parenting plan. (A parenting plan is a court document that allows either parent to request time with the child or children, which usually happens when one parent withholds a child from the other for a prolonged period without good cause. Once the requesting parent has filled out the paperwork and gone through the proper procedures, the case goes before the judge and the judge decides.)

This process can be a significant stumbling block to many of our clients. Most of these men have a past criminal history; they live with a great deal of distrust and shame. It's painful to have to list their offenses and failures on paper and have them repeated, judged again, and risk rejection. Many of them are only now, at this point, coming to realize how dysfunctional their lifestyle has been and how inhospitable that lifestyle is to a child.

Turning Things Around

Jeanett and I know firsthand how it feels to be labeled as "unfit parents." On one hand, we deserved it while we were in the madness of our addiction to crack. However, for people who are trying to turn their life around for the sake of their children, the label is counter productive.

As I began to walk in the straight life, which I will define as being married with my children in my home and earning an honest living, something like a fresh Seattle spring started to happen within me. For the first time in my entire life, I had the opportunity to give something back to my community rather than take from it. As strange as this may seem, I had never considered that the lifestyle I had been living was self-destructive until I looked into the eyes of my own children. It was then easy to see what other men were in the process of doing to their children by continuing to make the choices they were making.

I was slowly able to see that when I was in the devil's hands, I rose to the ranks of being a general in his army. I had a talent for convincing people to do wrong. Every day, I convinced people to take a chance on their lives to satisfy my own whims and desires. Amazingly, God mercifully saved me and turned me to use that same talent of persuasion to help people do *right*. He changed me from guiding people to what would be destructive to pointing them to what would be constructive. All of the things that I had done, and needed to continue to do to get on a healthy path, were things Jeanett and I could teach others to do. They were transferable.

For example, my Uncle Larron Patton humbly came to me in his addiction and asked me to help him go through the same steps I had gone through, so he could get his life on track. He was our first client at D.A.D.S. His life today is a walking miracle. He is now a man who has a strong walk with God, a successful career, and a rich relationship with his children—all because he was willing to do whatever he needed to do to connect with his children.

My nephew Terence, who was shot in the back and is now partially paralyzed, came to me one day and said, "Uncle, I have seen how you and Auntie have turned your lives around. Will you help me change my life?" It was a privilege to share my "faith" with him, not the whole gospel message, but my faith. I just told him how I trusted God one step at a time and he could do the same thing.

It was an advantage that these people knew me in my past. They knew there wasn't anything special about me, but that it was God who was doing the changes in me. Terence, my sister Marion's eldest child, was like a son to me. He traveled with me when I was in the Game and was attracted to the fast-money lifestyle. I take responsibility for some of the choices he made because he was imitating me. How glad and relieved I am that he has also imitated my repentance and faith—and is living a productive and responsible life in his adult years. Terence is now a program manager for the Union Gospel Mission in Seattle.

When a man is in recovery from drug addiction, or is coming out of prison and seeking to live a changed, productive life that includes being a positive influence on his child, he needs to feel hope that he can do this. The last thing he needs is for someone to heap more shame upon him; he already feels it. What he needs is hope and practical tools. Jeanett and I are living, breathing examples that it can actually be done! And because we have done it, we can point the way to others.

For the father in this chapter's opening story, this is exactly what happened. Realizing he wasn't in a place to parent his son full time, he made the emotionally difficult (but ultimately wise) decision to return the boy to his mother. However, he immediately started to make the necessary arrangements to bring his son to live with him in the future. As we walked him through the process, we also coached him in some personal growth areas:

1. He applied for and implemented a parenting plan.
2. He found a steady job.
3. He obtained suitable housing.
4. He learned to communicate with legal personnel in a respectful and professional manner.
5. He learned to walk "the straight life."

That's not as easy as it may sound to some readers. It's overwhelming for these men to all at once seek a stable job (especially if they are convicted felons), decent housing, and a clean, sober, and safe life, and to start to repair the wreckage of their past. For some, this becomes a reality/spirit check. They realize they really aren't ready to take on the responsibility of being a full-time parent. But even when this is the case, we encourage them to stay in the race, start putting the pieces of their life in order (that's what we're here for), and move forward toward making their dream of parenting a reality. After all, we frequently tell these clients, "Doing something beats whining and complaining about what isn't happening!" Our heart's desire is to give them hope. If you can give a person hope, it's amazing how much more that person will aspire to do on his own!

Turning the Tide on Fatherlessness

The stories you've read are but a few of the many we've experienced at D.A.D.S., and our numbers speak for themselves. Over the last 14 years, D.A.D.S. has assisted over 3,000 men in becoming fathers again—not just biologically, but relationally and practically. These men have been reunited with over 6,100 children. Extrapolating the social cost savings associated with these 3,000+ individuals, D.A.D.S. saved the State of Washington millions of dollars over the last 14 years. And, there is a larger story.

Our numbers are best illustrated by stories like that of William, who was raised by his father from an early age to survive on the street through criminal activity. As a result, William lived with 17 aliases, multiple children, multiple women, multiple incarcerations, and the accumulation of over $100,000 in unpaid child support. This set of conditions is typical of D.A.D.S. clients when they walk through our doors for the first time.

Ironically, William found D.A.D.S. based on the mistaken belief from "word on the street" that D.A.D.S. would help him avoid the obligation to pay child support. Our team welcomed William with open arms as we do every new D.A.D.S. client. As time went on, William found that instead of avoiding child support responsibility, his D.A.D.S. experience helped him learn the importance of living in community and assuming responsibility, not only for child support but also for his entire life. We helped William establish a parenting plan that allowed him to make regular child support payments and establish regular visitation with his children. In the process, William discovered hope for a new future. And, like so many others, the love William had for his children became a profound motivation to break the generational cycle of incarceration and destructive behavior.

During this period, William demonstrated a knack for fixing computer hardware and software applications and applied those skills to a small business as a computer service handyman. He began attending community college and studied IT. Simultaneously, William was helping other D.A.D.S. clients navigate the same process he did. He also became the driving force behind a group of D.A.D.S. former clients who run a successful mentor program at a city alternative school for youth at risk of drug abuse, street violence, teen pregnancy, dropping out of school, and incarceration.

William went on to graduate from community college with a degree in IT. Upon graduation, he applied for a job with a corporate executive he met through his work at D.A.D.S., and is now a highly respected IT professional at one of Seattle's most recognized companies. He is married, in relationship with his children, is a homeowner, and pays taxes. Instead of being supported by society, he supports others. In January of 2015, William Hughes was elected as President of the Board of Directors of D.A.D.S.

Without D.A.D.S., William would have continued to search for ways to avoid his unpaid child support, thereby continuing to live his life on the perimeter of society and ultimately returning to incarceration, separation from his children, and self destructive behavior. Instead, he is now a loving, responsible husband, father, and citizen, and a driving force to help other men like him overcome their past, navigate "the system," re-establish an active parent relationship with their children, and forge a brighter future for themselves and their families.

Working with the System

For men like William, it is key that they learn to work toward recovery and restoration within the established legal and welfare system. "The System" is the interplay of different governmental agencies that a father must navigate in order to gain access to—and eventually custody of—his children, if that is the objective. In our home state of Washington, there is the DSHS (Department of Social and Health Services), TANF (the federal welfare program), CPS (Child Protective Services), and of course Family Court. These agencies all work closely together. CPS recommends to the court whatever it decides "on the ground," based on home visits and information collected on the father and his family situation. (The court will nine times out of ten go along with the social worker's recommendation.) The whole system works together to do one thing, to protect the child. That goal I totally agree with, but how they go about achieving this objective is what I sometimes have a problem with.

The system runs on the compilation of information. If a father does not carefully keep a record of *every positive move* he is making towards being responsibly involved with his children, even if he is not living with them, he remains at a tremendous disadvantage. I cannot emphasize this strongly enough. A man can either rail against this system or he can learn to work within it. Jeanett and I have learned to work within it, and that is the knowledge we pass on to the dads we help. What we learned was by trial and error. We give our men the advantage of our experience of *working within the system.*

How It Works

Let's say a man comes into our office and complains that he is not able to visit his child. In order for his voice to be heard (legally), he needs to be able to present a parenting plan to the court. One thing we do, on a case-by-case basis, is look at each father and determine realistically what kind of plan he should propose to the judge in order to have the best chance of being accepted. Should it be a full-time or part-time parenting plan? First, the judge is going to look at the man to see if he is paying child support. If he is not, he might as well not go to court.

We help the father see this as a long-term process that will require him to put some things in place. Often, as we mentioned earlier, this necessitates a harsh reality check. Once we get a man to this place, and he begins to understand the real challenge he is facing, then we can gradually build him up with hope, the same hope that sustained us through many setbacks in bringing our own family back together.

Many fathers, once they see where they really are, will say something like, "I'm not ready yet to go to court." They start to fathom that no job + no house = no kids. They grasp their situation and put their energies into finding a job and then securing some affordable housing.

Once a father gets a job, any job, he can begin to make payments on his child support. We urge him to comply with the minimum on everything so he can demonstrate to the judge that he is operating in good faith. We recommend a child support payment he can afford, and the minimum amount of time that the judge will likely allow. We want the man to build a track record of success, of fulfilling his obligations and making incremental progress.

Understanding Child Support Obligations

A part of the incremental progress needed will be a man's ability to fulfill his child support obligations. Sadly, most of these men aren't even aware of how they got into the child support system to begin with, which often leads to a great deal of frustration.

Here's how it commonly happens: A man's girlfriend gets pregnant and goes to the TANF office (Temporary Aid for Needy Families), where she receives medical coupons, and food stamps to support her until the baby is born. She also receives a stipend to sustain her while she's pregnant. Often a father is not even aware that this is happening, even if he is living in the home.

But, before she can receive the coupons and stipend, the woman must identify the father. The DSHS office (Department of Social and Health Services) passes the man's name on to the Prosecuting Attorney's office, which sends out a letter to the man confirming that he is the father of the woman's child. There is often no response as the man is transient or doesn't check his mail. However, if there is not a response, the PA office assigns a wage (a right granted to the states by the federal government), that it takes from a standardized chart, and a corresponding child support payment.

For example, if a man is deemed eligible to earn 5,000 dollars a month, the State will take 1,000 dollars a month (or whatever amount is assigned, and then immediately places that man in an "arrears" category, and the debt begins to accumulate. This builds month after month, year after year, until the man decides he wants to find a job and live the straight life. To his shock and horror, the first paycheck will be nearly nothing—because the government knows his Social Security number and immediately garnishes the wage.

This is where I believe systems break up families. The reason I say this is because, now, who is the first person the father is going to blame? It's the mother of his child. He will reason, "She turned me into child support!" – although she didn't really have a choice. In reality, his poor understanding of the system and his failure to respond to the PA's correspondence are more accurately to blame, but he generally doesn't realize that. This scenario happens over and over and over.

Take William, for example. He owed $100,000 because, like most of these men, he had no idea how the system actually works. They see no way of getting out of it. They can't even do a parenting plan if they aren't paying child support. In futility, they often say, "Why should I pay child support; I don't get to see my kids anyway!" But the reality is, if you don't pay child support, you can't start on the parenting plan.

Practical and Spiritual Realities

We counsel men to turn from blame and resentment, and from what can be a confrontational, vindictive situation that pits father against mother in the courtroom, to a cooperative effort to do what is best for the child. Once the judge sees that is where the father is coming from, he or she will be more likely to grant the father's request.

Once the father has a track record of compliance, some steady employment, and is addressing any other issues that need attention, he needs to make a compilation of data, documenting and proving that he is actively addressing those problems. Let's say the father has been accused by his wife or girlfriend of being a drug user, or physically abusive. He must be able to present tangible proof that he is addressing the issue. If it is drug use, he needs to show a track record of attending rehab and submitting to UA (Urine Analysis). If the issue is abuse, he needs to show a record of attendance to classes or therapy for the issue. He needs to learn how to file his own paperwork and represent himself with facts before the family court judge. When he receives a court date and appears before the judge, the judge will usually say, "If you do _____, we will allow you to do _____. " At that point, the father begins to follow the direction of the court.

I use the term "courtroom etiquette" to describe to a man how he needs to approach the court environment and personnel. He needs to conduct himself with dignity, not speak out of turn, and not retaliate emotionally to courtroom proceedings. He must treat everyone in the room with honor, and let his paperwork speak for itself. This demonstrates respect for the judge and the system. Then I encourage him to be patient and watch God work!

Though the processes through which we guide these men are very practical and often technical, Jeanett and I have come to learn that "everything is spiritual." The Bible tells us our battles are often "not against flesh and blood but against the spiritual forces of evil" in this world (Ephesians 6:11-18). That's why we named our organization "DIVINE Alternatives for Dads Services."

I was facing a situation when I was 43 years old that could not be overcome by my own willpower, or my own wisdom—it took God. Jesus Christ began to set me free and put me on a path that was no longer digging myself into a hopeless pit. Now I lead other men in repeating their own version of my story. For me, it isn't just a one-time event that happened years ago; it is an ever-unfolding story, an ongoing struggle, and a commitment to continue to walk and learn with others who are traveling the same path. This gives them permission to struggle, too—to not pretend they have arrived, because at D.A.D.S. we don't pretend that we have. That's how I try to lead, with transparency: I am on the same path they are and I understand the battle, because I am in it every day with them.

We have a group that meets in my office every Wednesday morning, and every Thursday evening for men who are working during the day. The daytime group in particular is a very diverse group that includes men "from park bench to Park Avenue." Every Wednesday black, white, rich, poor, old, young, ex-cons, retired CEOs, recovering addicts, and model citizens gather together at the level ground of the cross of Jesus Christ. It is there that men who are moving towards responsible fatherhood can learn from other men and gain the support they need to persevere in the journey. It is here, most importantly, that they discover they are not alone. As we read and discuss the Gospels together, they learn that Jesus is with them and has given them brothers who want to stand with them in friendship and prayer.

I emphasize to the men with whom we work the importance of having a *personal* relationship with Jesus. In the African American culture, a history of churchgoing among men is common but a personal relationship with God is not. When they are exposed to men around the circle reading the Bible and sharing life together, they realize that followers of Jesus are not just a bunch of "Bible thumpers." This is a paradigm shift that often ends up radically transforming not only a man, but also an entire family.

Shep's Story

Shep found D.A.D.S. in one of the most unlikely of ways—he was shot outside the front door in a domestic dispute, an incident that landed him in prison for six months on a felony charge. It was years later that different circumstances brought him back to our front door.

When Shep showed up at D.A.D.S., he introduced himself and told Jeanett, who was at the front counter that day, that he wanted visitation with his children, whom he hadn't seen in two years. He had been looking at his parenting plan online and wasn't sure how to attack it. In his own words, "Government paperwork, for someone who's been avoiding the legal system his whole life, is pretty intimidating."

Shep first became a father when he was still in high school;

he was just 18 years old when his son was born, followed by two daughters over the years. Although he had a presence in his children's lives, he was not an active parent. For one, he didn't really know how.

"My dad had things going on in the other room, you know," Shep explains simply. "I didn't get any of the tools from my own parents for how to raise kids—like how to communicate, figure things out, or how to assert myself appropriately. Mostly my dad taught me to stay as far as I could from the law. I didn't realize at the time that the law was there *for* me, as well."

Shep was only ten years old when gangs from California migrated north to Seattle, where he lived. "We weren't safe in our own neighborhood, having lunch or walking to school. So we joined the gangs to protect ourselves." And that was how life went, for many years. Shep stayed away from the hard drugs because he saw what they did to everyone else. Alcohol was his drug of choice; it dulled the pain of losing his parents and being estranged from his children. "I didn't know what to do with my emotions," Shep explains in retrospect.

At D.A.D.S., Shep was invited to join the Thursday night men's group as he was learning to navigate the system and fill out his paperwork. Even though spirituality was not something he'd ever been too interested in, Shep showed up. He candidly told the group what he'd been going through – depression, alcoholism, and trying to have some focus, hold down his job, and get his kids back.

We told Shep what we tell other clients in his situation: that's not going to work! Shep needed that harsh reality check I mentioned earlier. If he were going to go about this the same way he'd approached everything else in his life, nothing would change.

But if he would be willing to change his thinking, even the way he carried and presented himself, and the way he parented—if he were willing to do some learning and listening – it could happen. There were some steps he had to take. So Shep quit drinking, and for the first time in a long time, his head cleared.

Jeanett's first recommendation to Shep with regard to his parenting plan was to invite his ex-wife to fill out the paperwork with him. "Are you kidding?" Shep asked incredulously. "She won't even take my calls." Jeanett urged him to try. To Shep's utter amazement, the children's mother agreed. They met at D.A.D.S., sat down at a table, and came up with a parenting plan. Ultimately, she didn't follow through with her end of the deal. But Shep's efforts had been enough. "I took the class, I went through all the steps, I did everything they asked of me. They said I could have even more visitation than I asked for!"

Next, Shep joined AA. As he got his family together, he started getting his life together, too. "Once I stopped drinking and positive things were happening in my life, something hit me. It was God. My spiritual life started exploding; I even got baptized. Things started going right!"

Admittedly, Shep says the reunion with his daughters was no easy thing. "When I got the girls, it was difficult at first because we were a bit foreign to each other. I was confused about how to care for the needs of young women. My toughness and thick skin made it hard for them to talk to me; I had to learn to listen. It was slow progress at first. But it keeps getting better. And they call me now, just out of the blue. We even had a family vacation this summer."

Shep spoke at our annual D.A.D.S. banquet last spring, held in Seattle. The crowd was riveted by his powerful testimony of restoration. But no one was prouder than Shep's daughters, seated in the audience and cheering on their dad!

Hope—Even When It Feels Hopeless

Shep's story is but one of hundreds like it that Jeanett and I hear regularly. We can relate as well as rejoice, because we have the unique perspective of having had to learn to navigate the system ourselves and learn to make it work for us, not against us. We learned it, as I've said earlier, through trial and error, because there was NO way around it. (Granted, there are many flaws in this system, which made—and continue to make—it very difficult to navigate. That, perhaps, is a topic for another book!)

When we were trying to bring our family together and get back on our feet, Jeanett and I were both in the situation of being assessed far more damages in back child support than we could possibly have paid at that point in time. When we finally secured jobs, after getting clean and feeling like we were making so much progress, the system came after us for half our wages. That was a crushing blow, especially while we were making such great strides to get our lives back on track, and to generate the income we needed to get established. We felt totally helpless.

Fortunately, we had some fair caseworkers who worked with us to see the processes through, versus telling us there wasn't anything they could do (which frequently happens). They would send us documents to complete and return, and shared what could possibly happen if we did things right. That was the hope we needed to press on.

Jeanett will never forget her final conference board hearing where they reviewed her history, re-evaluated her income, and recalculated her debt. At the end of the hearing, the decision was granted to charge off all debt. Jeanett will tell you today with a grin, "My debt was paid in FULL; I didn't owe another dime! I had all my babies at home and I was clean and sober. I was able to continue to rebuild my new life."

Our story encourages men and women to know that sometimes it's not what we've done but what we don't do that prevents us from moving forward. This is the motto we work from: GIVE HOPE. We always want to communicate the hope of possible change to counteract the feeling of despair, that hopeless feeling that "there is nothing that can be done." D.A.D.S. clients—both fathers and mothers—find hope in just having someone say, "We will work this out with you." Once we empower them with a little information, they start to thirst and hunger for more.

CHAPTER TEN
Hope and Help for the Journey

Mac was a 26-year-old father of two children under five who came to us after serving some felony jail time and working a few menial jobs after he got out of prison. When Mac requested help in connecting with his children, I challenged him to take some serious steps. I helped him get a car and provided a place for him to live until he got a job and got on his feet, which he did. We encouraged him to begin sending money to the mother of his children. This was his chance to create his own environment, take responsibility, and be empowered to make changes. Unless he did this, we counseled him, he would never be able to become involved in his children's life.

The reality is—for Mac and every other man in his situation— that the mother of his child(ren) is in contact with the Division of Child Support (DCS). If the father of her child has been acting irresponsibly, that information will be well documented. A debt is being racked up. Unless he shows some goodwill and effort toward compliance, he doesn't have much of a chance in getting a break from Family Court.

I told Mac, as I tell all the men who come to us, "Give yourself two years to create something, to get some work history, to get on a program where your kids can be on your medical insurance if possible. This is the foundation you need, something you can build on." I also told him, "You've got to put yourself to the side and let go of 'you,' and start doing 'them.'" I find myself saying this a lot.

Very often, the man does not naturally grasp what it is going to take for him to become involved in his children's lives in a healthy, positive way. Most of these men have never really considered (or even seen modeled) what it looks like to be in a caring, reciprocal relationship where they give sacrificially for another person's well-being. That's not to say they don't want to learn. But most of them have lived their whole lives in circumstances that have created a worldview and mindset that perpetuates self-serving behaviors. Many if not most of them, out of what felt like necessity, have grown up with an attitude of survival and self-interest, and this translates into their most personal relationships. It takes time, relational investment, training, and life-to-life role modeling—"walking alongside"—to help them learn these life lessons. But it can and does happen!

Building Healthy Relationships

Karl came into our office and explained to Jeanett that he was having difficulty with "his woman." However, because of his immature and self-centered concept of relationships, I believe he couldn't even hear what Jeanett had to say. I began to try to give him some counsel in his situation.

It turned out that, very soon after his girlfriend had their baby, there arose a conflict of vision about what it means to have a child. It was not even on his radar that anything would change in their relationship after she gave birth to the child. Of course, in Karl's mind, it was all about how she related (or not) to *him*.

What Karl was not appreciating is that there are significant changes in a woman's body, mind, and emotions after she has a baby, that we as men will never understand. She has carried the baby for nine months and is heavily invested in the child, and rightly so. But as she goes through the hormonal and emotional changes after the birth of the baby, the energy she used to have may not be there. She may be irritable or emotional. This is natural. But many of the men we see at D.A.D.S. don't recognize this. Very often, this woman's boyfriend will reject her. He will likely resort to other comforting mechanisms that he has used in the past when he felt lonely or rejected. He may drift into a relationship with another woman. This, of course, shuts down the mother of his child. It makes it highly unlikely that she will want the father involved in her child's life—and the biggest loser is the child.

When Karl came to our office, he was under the impression from different fathers' rights groups that all he needed to do was get a lawyer who could convince a judge that it was his right to get half the time with his child. What he didn't understand was how the legal system worked. No judge would separate a mother from her child while she was breastfeeding. His best opportunity to have extended time with his child was when the boy was somewhere between three and five years old. The best thing Karl could do was to renegotiate the relationship between himself and the mother so it was not confrontational, and then take advantage of every opportunity in those first one to three years to bond with his son.

What Karl and men like him must understand—and need help with—is that if a concerted effort isn't made toward intentionally fathering, then the chances are that by the time he would legally have an opportunity, he will be alienated from his child. So what I tell a man is, besides seeking to bond with his child, he needs to create a healthy environment with a job, and a home into which he can invite his son or daughter at the right time. He needs to provide a documented means of support for the child.

"Hey Marvin, would you do me a favor?" Karl asked me one day. "Would you call her for me? She isn't answering my texts."

I answered him, "Yes, but I want you to do something first. Tell her that you have re-thought what you were doing and that you were wrong. You need to tell her you're sorry." When he did that, I told him, I would attempt the call and get back to him. He followed through, I called, and she responded. Karl needed guidance through the relational steps required, not just the legal steps. This is what walking alongside men looks like.

It Takes a Village

The real ministry of D.A.D.S. is not what we do in our services for men but in the ways that God transforms people. We live in such an information culture; mere words have lost their impact. What really impacts hearts is when faith and hope put on hands and feet.

Bob is a man in his early forties who went to prison for 16 years, entering the correctional system almost 20 years ago for selling drugs. He had two children in another state. After he served 128 months, his sentence was commuted to 90 months, so he was immediately released. He now wants to live a normal life and re-connect with his children.

I let Bob's situation be known among our donors and those who own or are in leadership positions in companies. These are people who believe in what D.A.D.S. is doing and understand that men like Bob need a support system around him, men who can walk alongside him as well as someone who can offer him a work opportunity. These people understand not only the depth of the battle these men face, but also the healing power of Jesus at work through ordinary people. They trust the combination of practical steps we help men take in working through the system, and the power of support that comes from our weekly Bible study.

As we walk someone like Bob through his paperwork, or give a man like Karl some counsel in relating to his child's mother, we invite him to walk with the other men who are going through the same process, or have walked through it and are on the other side. The power of D.A.D.S. is for these men to see other men's lives transform, often in their attitudes first and then in their situations. They are not being told to change, but they are watching other men change and learning how to walk the same path. Success stories beget more success stories.

It is not only what men like Bob see when they go to the groups, but also what they are able to process and express themselves through their journey—that they are not alone. That keeps them encouraged to persevere on a healthy course. They see how a walk of faith and intentional fatherhood is lived out, however imperfectly, by men like themselves.

Learning to Be a Father

More than anything else, it is developing positive relationships with their children that encourages and motivates men to lead more constructive lives. However, most of the men we see have no idea how to BE a father.

For one thing, most of them have had very little contact, or at least irregular contact, with their children up to this point. According to a Pew Research Center Report, about half of fathers who don't live with their kids only see their children a few times a year, or have no visits at all. In addition, almost one-third of those fathers correspond with their kids over the phone or via email less than once a month.[31] Roughly one-in-five fathers who live apart from their children say they visit with them more than once a week, and an additional 29% see their children at least once a month. For 21% of these fathers, the visits take place several times a year. And for 27% there are no visits at all.

When it comes to spending time with a child and learning how to parent, being in the same home with the child makes a huge difference. According to the same Pew Research report, more than nine in ten fathers who live with their children at least part of the time report they share a meal with their child or talk with him or her about the child's day almost daily. Nearly two-thirds (63%) say they help their child with homework or check on their homework at least several times a week, and 54% say they take their child to or from activities several times a week or more.

By comparison, relatively few fathers who live apart from their children report taking part in these activities. Imagine when the fathers get custody, or begin participating regularly in parenting activities, how ill equipped they feel. This is another area where a supportive community can provide support and resources.

What Struggling Dads Need to Know

There are plenty of good resources available to teach men how to be good dads. But the men we see find themselves in a different situation from the average person in the general population who simply wants to improve his parenting skills, who already has at least a foundational understanding of what it means to be a dad. Most of the men we see—who have come through the prison system, who have spent their lives in dysfunctional family settings, on the streets, or who have never had an involved dad themselves (many of our D.A.D.S. dads relate to all these categories simultaneously)—have no idea what it looks like to be a good father.

The problems are huge. The stakes are high. And the journey ahead is long. But it's all worth the effort and investment—to a single child, and potentially to an entire nation.

BECOMING DADS

CHAPTER ELEVEN
Becoming the Dad a Child Needs

When Jeanett and I got married, the home we formed was a blended family. The children we had living with us at the time included my son Marvin Jr. (10) and daughter Lyric (5), Jeanett's son Jeffery (7), and Devotion (4) and Marvette (2), who were ours. From all appearances, things looked really good; but in reality, there was lots of tension.

Jeanett and I always seemed to be doing this uncomfortable dance. Marvin Jr. was "my son" and Jeffery was "her son" and resentment started to build towards each other about how we parented our children. For my part, I was resorting to parenting methods I had learned from my uncle E.J. Marvin Jr. was now exactly the same age I had been when I entered my uncle's home, and I found myself trying to father him in the way Uncle E.J. fathered me, though not as extreme. The shadow of Uncle E.J., that of a "false father," haunted me. I was promoting fatherhood through D.A.D.S, becoming recognized, and looking good on the outside. But on the inside, in my own home, I was resorting to the parenting model I had experienced.

I knew I had drawn from this dark side of me when I was in "the life." I knew I had learned well to control others through my mouth, through threats and intimidation. As I began to face the challenges in my own home, I am ashamed to say that I resorted to Uncle E.J.'s ways, especially toward my son. I was becoming a respected fatherhood advocate in the community and I so much longed to be an example for other fathers to follow, but I was blowing it in my own family.

I took training courses for fathering but there was a big difference between what I knew in my head I should do, and what was going on in my heart in the heat of the battle. It seemed that when the pressure was on, I resorted to what I knew, even if I recognized deep down it was the same destructive form of fathering I'd fled when I was sixteen. I tried to rule my children with intimidation. If they messed up, I would revert to abusive sayings I learned on the street.

As Marvin Jr. progressed through middle school, I became obsessed with the ways he was falling short. I verbally abused him and it started getting physical. All I could think of was how was I going to get this out of him. I wanted to protect him from the lifestyle Jeanett and I had come out of. My motives were right, but my methods were all wrong.

One day after I had whipped Marvin with a belt, Jeanett came to me and said, "Why do you go on whipping your son so hard?" We both believed that there was a place for corporal punishment but she knew I had crossed a line. One day, he went to school after a whipping and a teacher saw welts on his arm. One of his teachers called Child Protective Services (CPS).

When Jeanett heard this, she started wailing, "No, no, they aren't going to take our kids away again!" She was inconsolable, holding Marvette and Devotion like they were still babies.

I walked into Marvin and Jeffery's room and saw Marvin with a rope around his neck. This is when I finally realized I had done something terribly wrong, and that I couldn't keep on doing this. I had to change the way I fathered Marvin. I put my arms around him and cried. I told him I loved him, and that I wanted him to become a better person but I had gone about it the wrong way. I explained to him how CPS worked.

"Son, CPS will take you out of this home if they think you are in danger. Do you realize that?" He didn't. I knew they hadn't told him that fact.

A couple of days later, we received a letter from CPS, notifying us that they would keep our case open for the next six years. This was a low point for me. But it reinforced in me the realization that it is a *battle* to change a generational curse of fatherlessness, to reverse the curse of a false father—an abusive father—and to learn to become a true father, a nurturing father. It is a battle we must win. And, like real warfare against an entrenched enemy, there are no easy victories.

A Better Path

A good friend of mine says, "Jesus hangs out at the end of ropes," and that is where I met "Jesus" with skin on, in one Art Kopicky. Art had approached me about wanting to "walk with me," and at the time I didn't understand what he meant. Now, as I was going through deep struggles with my own fatherhood, I began to confide in him about the challenges I was facing. He wasn't over me like a boss nor was he under me like an employee; he was a friend, just walking alongside. That was what I needed.

I told Art about my difficulties being a father to Marvin Jr., and the challenges Jeanett and I were experiencing in trying to raise a blended family. He listened well and prayed with me. I felt relief that I wasn't alone. I asked him what he did in certain situations in his family. I watched his example as a father and I slowly began to learn a better path, a way that wasn't about controlling my children as Uncle E.J. had done with me, but about leading them through listening to them and winning their hearts.

One day, after we had spent time together in my living room, Art put his hands on my shoulders, looked me in the eyes, and said, "Marvin, you are my beloved son, in whom I am well pleased," repeating the blessing that God the Father had spoken over His Son, Jesus, after His baptism in the Jordan River.[32] I had never been validated like that as a son of the heavenly Father. Something inside of me broke. As soon as I could, I did the same with my sons Marvin Jr. and Jeffery, both in their teens by this time. Art was a vessel that spoke the Father's blessing to me, and I could feel the cold, dark curse of Uncle E.J. begin to melt away from the warm, embracing light that came from this blessing.

I also confided in Art about my relationship with Jeanett and my struggles in being the husband I really wanted to be, but that I wasn't able to be through my best efforts. He opened my eyes to the importance of patience—with my wife, with my children, and with the ministry of D.A.D.S.. He also helped me listen to the parenting wisdom that was coming from Jeanett. She had been raised by a single father, a good and faithful man named Tommy Jones.

"Marvin, your kids are people, too, with little minds of their own," Jeanett would say to me. This was hard for me to grasp, as I would see them as my uncle had modeled, as beings that needed to be shaped and controlled to conform to my rules. All I could eat, drink, and think was, "I don't want these kids to go down the road that Jeanett and I just came from. I have to protect them from all of that; I have to draw a line in the sand and make sure they don't cross it."

With Art and Jeanett's help, this is when I realized I needed to change my methods and started thinking, *How can I mentally get the message across instead of physically trying to get it across?* This greater understanding began to benefit me not only in my home and family, but also in my ministry on Sundays as the Sunday School Superintendant at my church.

The Sunday School started to grow and become packed out. Jeanett worked with me as the Sunday School secretary. My children became more involved in church, with the girls in the Angel Choir. We would sing praises in the car together. Some nights we would turn off the television and sing songs together. We began to experience a "spring" that was following the winter we had just experienced. In this season of my fatherhood, we would do all of our family activities together. I saw my friends like Art and Jamie do family activities together and I believed that we could do that, too, as a family. And we did.

Adopting a Healthy Parenting Model

Jeanett and I, along with our kids, started out right away attending the Atlantic Street Center in Seattle, a family oriented place where kids could hang out while their parents went to different groups to get what they needed. We enrolled in parenting classes and support groups. We learned a lot there. It also gave us many opportunities to share our own story of hope.

For people who had good parenting role models growing up, there is a higher likelihood that they will have a healthier parenting style. But if a person's models were poor, then it is going to take a more concentrated effort to learn to parent lovingly and effectively. Of course, that is a generalization; however, it is fairly true most of the time.

One reason for this is a scientific term, "homeostasis," which basically means *by default we will tend to revert back to a consistent pattern of behavior.* That pattern of behavior is usually what was modeled for us when we were growing up. But what is important to remember is that we are not doomed to repeat our past. We can change it!

To parent in a way that is different than how your parents did it is difficult. It takes an intense amount of effort and willpower to break the mold and consistently do things in a different way. *You have to get past your past.* You have to gain momentum to jump over the hurdle of poor parenting styles you saw modeled in your childhood.

How can you get past your past and become a healthy role model for your own children? Here are some ways to start:

1. Identify any positive aspects of your parents' parenting. These were perhaps never verbalized but you know them because you can recognize what was effective in how they parented you. Jeanett had some very positive principles modeled for her by her dad and these were a great help to both of us.

2. Identify the negative things your parents taught you or modeled for you that were not good parenting skills.

These must be identified, and discussed with your spouse if you are married, to give you support and accountability to make sure they are extinguished from your parenting repertoire.

3. Forgive.

This is an important step. If there was abuse or injustice in your own childhood experience, you must, with God's help, release the anger and bitterness that may be built up inside you. Forgiveness doesn't mean you are saying it was okay. It does mean you are releasing your hold on the past and trusting God to deal with that person or people justly. When you forgive, the person who goes free is you.

4. Find a support community or person.

This is huge. For us, it was the Atlantic Street Center and our church, and people like Art Kopicky and my friend Jamie Bohnett. Find people and places where you can observe and be reinforced in healthy parenting models.

5. Take parenting classes.

It may feel humbling, invasive, and even intrusive at first to let strangers into this part of your life, but it is what you must do if you really want to learn and grow.

A New Mindset

As my children grew into adulthood, my new parenting skills were frequently put to the test. For example, with my boys, as young African American men growing up in a large city, there were a number of pitfalls and problems I felt constantly compelled to try to keep them away from. But as I'd recognized early on, I had to learn to get my messages across *mentally* instead of *physically*.

There was the battle to get them to pull up their pants. Now, you can punish your children; you can tell them to pull up their pants, but they have to understand why. For me, it was more than a matter of fashion. This is what I wanted my sons to understand, from my experience:

> *You see, son, "sagging" will attract the attention of the police, who then want to know who you are, in case you are a potential future violator. So, when they spot you, a potential candidate (identified by something like "sagging"), they might charge you for something simple, like jaywalking. On the streets, they call this "jacking you up"—they look you up, see if you're in the system, and take note of you in case they ever see you again. For your part, you are embarrassed, don't tell your parents, and don't pay the ticket. But then, when you are 18, that warning turns into a warrant. Now the police have reason to arrest you for real, fingerprint you, and put you in "the system."*
>
> *So, do you see now, son, why I want you to pull up your pants?*

Now, ultimately, I can't follow my sons around and make sure their pants are pulled up! But can you see how my methods have changed from heavy-handedness to logic? This is an important part of the process of developing a new parenting mindset.

Developing Dads

We realized at D.A.D.S. that an important part of the process of restoring absent fathers would be teaching them to actually "become dads." For this, my friend Jamie Bohnett connected me to the National Center for Fathering, a faith-based fathering training organization out of the Kansas City area. NCF had been an organization with whom Jamie had done work the past ten years, and then-director Dr. Ken Canfield had become a mentor and friend to him. NCF was aware of the great need for fatherhood training among urban fathers and was just beginning to formulate training targeted to this population.

Jamie wanted me to meet Ken but also wanted Ken to meet me and some others, so his family's foundation sponsored a NCF training seminar for men who worked with fathers in the Seattle area. Jamie recruited a group of seven men to receive the training, based upon Dr. Ken Canfield's excellent book for fathers, *Seven Secrets for Effective Fathering*.

As the seminar began, I was skeptical. There were examples that I knew would not apply to the men I was working with, who were coming out of the hood. But what brought me up short was a question Ron Nichols, the facilitator, asked us: "Can you tell me the names of your children's best friends?" I was stumped. I knew that my son, Marvin Jr., knew my friends' names but I hadn't taken the time to learn the names of his friends. Ron explained that by not knowing our kids' friends names, we were sending a message to them: we don't care enough to be aware of their world. I made sure that night I learned the names of my childrens' best friends!

Ron let me know about a new curriculum that the Center was coming out with called *Quenching the Father Thirst*, developed by Dr. George Williams. Eventually, it was made possible for me to go back to Kansas City and receive that training. It was there I met Dr. Ken Canfield, who became a mentor to me. The curriculum was right on target, discussing issues like "fatherless fathers" and "baby mama drama." I later repeated the training with several men from the community with Dr. George Williams facilitating. Now D.A.D.S. had a training piece in place to implement with our fathers.

What It Takes to Be a Good Dad

I want to take some space here to highlight a few of the most common and important parenting principles we emphasize with the men in our D.A.D.S. program. These are key to helping them overcome the patterns of their past and build healthy new ones for the future. These principles include:

1. Learning to appropriately express both negative and positive emotions, and to meet their children's emotional needs. Men in general, in our society, have been taught that it is appropriate to display certain emotions and supress others. However, many men, particularly those from disadvantaged or abusive upbringings, have suppressed and denied healthy emotions so long that they no longer recognize them, nor are they able to handle them in the lives of others around them, such as their women and children. This puts them—and their children—at an extreme disadvantage in life. Through training and practice, and often some healing, they can learn to become emotionally healthy and create an emotionally healthy environment for their children.

2. Communicating to connect with their children through speaking and active listening. Many of the men we work with are not parenting full time and need to learn to maximize the time they do have with their children. Relationships need to be culti-vated and nurtured, and we do that through communication, which includes the words we say, the tone we use, the body lan-guage we reflect, and the listening we do. As mentioned earlier, when I first started parenting my children full time, my commu-nication with them was geared toward getting them to comply with my wishes. Getting to know them as "little people" was a whole new experience for me, and required effort, training, and practice. Healthy communication with the goal of connecting emotionally with them was key.

3. Learning to engage with their children and entering their world through play and personal involvement. Being an involved dad means being intentional. It's not completely true that quality time beats quantity time. You've got to have enough quantity to get good quality! Fathers have the unique privilege of introduc-ing their children to the world and providing the safety and con-fidence for them to explore it. But if dads are uncomfortable with relating to their kids on the kids' level, this can be difficult. We help dads learn to play with their children at different levels, us-ing things like songs, stories, make believe, and simple games. As the children get older, this would include more complex games and activities, sports, hobbies, camping, fishing, road trips, and cooking or baking together.

This last point was key for me, and for us as a family. We needed to learn to play together and enjoy each other, and bond as a family. One time, a generous friend gave us the keys to a cabin his family owned up in LaConner, Washington, so we could have a vacation. We were able to go up there for a week and just play on the beach. We collected oysters, skipped rocks on the water, and played touch football on the beach. For one week we weren't about work but about play, and we were able to talk and dream of our future together.

Another significant time was when Jamie invited Marvin Jr. and me to join him and his son Jeremy to go down the Skykomish River on kayaks. I had never done that before. I was totally out of my element but Marvin and I actually survived the adventure—and enjoyed it! The next day I was so amazed at what we had done that I took my Uncle Larron for a drive up Highway 2 near Gold Bar and Sultan, where we had done this. These are things that families growing up urban Seattle just don't do. When we get a chance to do something like this, it is life-giving. It creates special family memories that we can treasure together, and that build a strong foundation for healthy relationships.

A Few of My "Dads' Don'ts"

Along the way, Jeanett and I also learned some "DON'Ts" as well as the "DOs" of good parenting. These were things that kind of snuck up on us, where we had an aha moment and realized some adjustments needed to made. I share them in the hopes that they will be helpful to any readers also walking this new parenting journey after coming out of a lifetime or even a season of unhealthy parental models:

1. Don't be a "helicopter parent." Some might think this is a problem primarily for the affluent, but this is not so. Because Jeanett and I wanted to make sure our kids didn't get gobbled up by what had consumed us, we tried to overprotect them. We lived in a potentially dangerous neighborhood; one night coming home from the Family Center, Jeanett's car was shot! So we were very careful, fearing any day a bullet could hit them and take their future. Our fear could have led to unreasonable restrictions, but we realized that this kind of mindset would cripple our children and leave them unable to cope with the realities of life on their own. You have to be willing to let them fight some adversity, take some responsibility, and endure some risk or discomfort sometimes. It won't break them; it will make them.

2. Don't try and make up for lost time. I got stuck on the years I missed, and was overwhelmed by shame and regret. This played out in how I related to my kids. Instead, now I think of the many years I have left to build a bright future. Here's a graphic illustration I used: I drew a timeline of my life, 0 to 80. I marked where, at 30, I became a biological father, and at 43, I became an intentional father. I can't recover those 13 years where I was living a destructive lifestyle that drastically impacted my children. However, I can see that I have 37 years or so after that—a far greater length of time—to make a substantial investment and impact on my children's lives. I must focus on this.

3. Don't spoil them. This is related to the two points above. At first, Jeanett and I tried to anticipate our kids' every need and disappointment and compensate for it. We wanted to give them what we hadn't had, or hadn't been able to provide, in the past. The problem was, it started to create an expectant spirit in them, an entitlement mentality. And it exhausted us, emotionally and financially! Don't over-give to win your children's hearts or make up for what happened in the past. Cell phones, Xboxes – these can become all-consuming and kids can start to shun you for these things; they become the focus and not the relationships in your household. Instead, give your kids experiences; the best outings are the ones that are new for you both.

4. Don't run from the system; teach them to navigate it.

For those who have been raised learning to distrust the law, authority, the legal system, etc., it can be a real challenge to learn to see these as positives in life and society. We need to teach our kids to respect and work with the system, even if we don't understand or like it.

I think that in urban culture, many times the only thing that people may feel they have left is their respect. They reason, "You've taken everything else from me, I'm not going to let you take my respect. I will fight like a caged animal for my respect." This is how we run into so many problems with reactions to authority.

When Jeanett and I first got our kids back and were assigned an extra six months of monitoring by CPS, I was angry and started to explode at the judge. Our caseworker restrained me and wisely encouraged me to work with it. So, we became inclusive and made a place for the "family preservation worker" appointed to us. She would be in our home while Jeanett prepared dinner and I was a support. She observed me speaking authoritatively but kindly to the kids in my interactions with them.

It was unique to incorporate this person who was coming into our home. I was already teaching parenting courses at the Family Center, so I took her with me, which created community with her and with the other parents, who were watching us navigate this whole process. It was a growing and learning process for all of us and really helped us start thinking of the "system" from a whole new perspective.

God's Grace Continues

In 2008, Jeanett spoke again to me two words I had heard twice before from her, so long ago, "Marvin, I'm pregnant." This was more than a surprise. I was 54 years old and Jeanett was 43. How was this going to work now at our age? Then I thought about a word that had been spoken over us in a church service, "God trusts you, Marvin and Jeanett." I thought to myself, *How can He trust me with my track record as a father? I haven't been a good father to my first seven children; how can He trust me with another?*

This child would be a beautiful little girl whom we would name Jamie-Michelle Dorothy Charles: Jamie, after my good friend Jamie Bohnett, Michelle, in honor of Michelle Obama, and Dorothy, to remember Jeanett's mother. Jamie would enter a family with a married mom and dad, who were clean and sober, part of the community, and givers not takers. This would be a whole new experience for one of my children, child number eight.

Eight children. Four sons, four daughters. By the miracle of God's grace, not one of them is following a criminal lifestyle. There is no crack cocaine addiction among them. Each of them understands the importance of hard work and education in varying degrees as you would expect with eight individuals with two fathers but five different mothers. I love them all and am proud of them all. I am believing and praying for each of them to find true success, that they would know God, and find His very best for their lives. I'm so very proud to be called ...

... their dad.

BECOMING DADS

ABOUT D.A.D.S.

If you look at our streets today, you'll see many young men and women looking for positive male role models. Mothers can do a lot, but children need their fathers. Without a strong male role model in their lives, they suffer in many ways.

As we've discussed, children of fatherless families have more behavior problems at school, and are more likely to enter the juvenile justice system. They do less well at school, and schools may have to make additional efforts to educate them. Additionally, their statistically higher use of drugs, alcohol, and tobacco, and poorer physical and mental health, may cause them to use mental health services more than children of two-parent families.[33]

The effects on children and families aside, the National Fatherhood Initiative has also identified fatherlessness as the root cause of **$100 billion a year in taxpayer costs**. According to the NFI, the federal government spent at least 99.8 billion dollars providing assistance to father absent families in 2006. In Washington State, the clients of D.A.D.S. reduced these costs to the state by 30%. If one extrapolates this percentage reduction across the United States, the reduction in costs would total approximately 30 billion dollars!

The Washington Department of Child Support compared its data base of over 80,000 men with unpaid child support debt to 2,700 D.A.D.S. clients. Here is what they found:

1. D.A.D.S. clients paid child support at a 29% higher rate (52%) versus non-DADS clients (41%).

2. D.A.D.S. clients reduced $36,000,000 in outstanding child support debt by $10,800,000, a 30% reduction.

3. D.A.D.S. clients increased their child support payments in one year such that the State of Washington saved over $1.24 million in TANF, Food Stamps, and Medicaid between September 2012 and October 2013.

D.A.D.S. has provided these services consistently for over 17 years without charging the client. These achievements are made possible by a combination of three factors:

- Assistance in navigating the system (parenting plans, child support, and child visitation)
- Helping to right size the imputed debt for unpaid child support
- Supportive community engagement with the fathers and their families

Our client population is predominantly non-white, and around 66% African American. About 90% have a history of incarceration. Since 2004, D.A.D.S. has provided *Quenching the Father Thirst* instruction to over 250 men in work-release programs at the Washington State Department of Corrections. That department reported that over the ten-year period from 2004 to 2014, NONE of those who completed the training had returned to prison.

For most of these men, the main motivation is the desire to reenter the lives of their children. Through the D.A.D.S. process, they are able to find and keep jobs, pay child support, purchase homes, and lead their families in ways that result in their children staying in school, off drugs, out of gangs, and going to college. Our statistics speak for themselves:

1. Since 2001, D.A.D.S. has provided weekly support group services to more than 2,000 men in Seattle and Tacoma, Washington. These groups give men critical coping and survival skills to relieve the stresses that place their families in danger of disintegration.

2. From 2001 to 2014, fathers in Washington State who were D.A.D.S. clients increased monthly child-support payments by 12%, according to the state's Division of Child Support (DCS).

3. From 2001 to 2014, fathers in Washington who were D.A.D.S. clients reduced the total amount of back child-support payments to their children by an additional $10.8 million, according to the DCS.

The effectiveness of the D.A.D.S. program depends on the trust that each individual develops in our staff, our process, and the community. We invest in building a vision for healthy fatherhood, in several different ways:

Navigating the system: D.A.D.S. helps men understand the process, forms, and documentation to successfully navigate the legal system related to child support, back payments, parenting plans, and visitation.

Treatment services: D.A.D.S. helps men find the support necessary to live lives that are drug and alcohol free.

Job/life skills training resources: D.A.D.S. trains men in personal leadership and life skills, and connects them to other training opportunities, as well.

Job sourcing assistance: Companies like Costco, Coastal Transportation, Fair Start, Pioneer Human Services, Upper Crust Catering, and others have hired D.A.D.S. clients.

Together We Can Turn It Around

It never fails to amaze me the many people who step up to play a role in this ministry, like Freddie, then a young University of Washington senior, who approached me about doing an internship with D.A.D.S. during his last year of college. He wanted to learn how we worked as a non-profit.

Freddie grew up in Redmond, an affluent eastside area of Seattle, and had a heart to be involved in helping the urban core of Seattle. He didn't really even know what he was getting himself into! His first week with us, he was waiting at the bus stop right outside of our office and doing some work on his MacBook Pro. A young African American man approached and asked him if he could look at his Facebook page on Freddie's laptop. Freddie agreed and let him take it. Once the young man had the computer in his possession, he indicated to Freddie that he was going to take it. Freddie got out his phone and said he was going to call the police. Thankfully, the young man backed down and gave Freddie his computer back, trying to cover his tracks. "I'm just messing with you man. I wasn't really gonna take your laptop!"

This was Freddie's rude awakening to life in the hood but it didn't throw him. He started doing menial work at D.A.D.S., like answering phone calls and taking messages. After Freddie became more familiar with our work doing intake, developing parenting plans, and approaching child support issues, he said he wanted to take a look at the data, our records, to see the impact that D.A.D.S. was having with families.

All of the records were accessible; since they were anonymous, no breach of confidentiality would be committed. He simply sought to see demographics, ages, ethnicity, gender, income, etc. of our clients. We handed over the documents and Freddie set to work.

About a month later, he came to us and said, "Do you realize how many people you have been helping here?" We had known we needed to collect data but we hadn't taken the next step and calculated it, allowing the data to speak and create a picture of the impact D.A.D.S. was having. Freddie was the one who showed us that over 6,100 children had become connected or re-united to their fathers through our efforts!

Armed with this knowledge, I went to Child Support Services to see if we had made a tangible difference with their clients. Freddie ran his numbers against what they were able to do at Child Support Services, and we shared those numbers with DCS. They were astonished! "The percentage of fathers we are able to see support their children is at 90%. Yours is at 88%." They couldn't believe how close we were to their percentage. (Through this, we—and they—recognized that we were reaching a population they had been unable to reach, because those individuals had shied away from interaction with the state and/or systems.)

The information that Freddie helped us attain enabled us to rally donor support in a way that we hadn't before. Before this, we had stories (anecdotal evidence) but now we had hard data to back up those stories. We had evidence on paper of what we'd seen with our eyes and felt in our hearts: we were making a difference!

Our ranks continue to swell with others who also want to make a difference. A father and son duo, Frank and Greg, traveled with us to Tijuana, Mexico during our now-annual house-building mission trip. A good friend of mine jokingly describes this colorful trip as "about 25 black and white men building houses together for a couple of brown families." On this excursion, men share their stories with each other and really bond as they are involved in doing something that is surely on Jesus' heart, helping the poor.

Frank is an architect and his 20-year old son, Greg, was a Washington State University student at the time. Frank developed an interest in our ministry, and started coming in mid-week to help out with various jobs around the office. When Greg came home from college, we offered him an internship. Like Freddie, Greg found a way he could help us through his talents. He was able to take the data Freddie had compiled and transform it into various graphs.

One graph stood out to me, the difference in the number of men we were able to help once we hired a full-time administrator and were able to keep our office open five days a week. We were able to help significantly more men by opening our doors just two more days a week!

What we were also able to see was that in the early days, the income level of the men we were able to help was averaging about $10,000 per year. Obviously, there was much unemployment and under-employment. But now, the range is more like $20,000 to $30,000. It is still largely low-income but now more of the men we help are fully employed. This data has huge implications for future fundraising and expanding D.A.D.S. offices throughout Washington State. We are currently praying and planning for a Tacoma office, and hoping that by 2025 we will have 10 D.A.D.S. locations throughout Washington State.

If you are in or around the Seattle area, we invite you to visit the D.A.D.S office at 5709 Rainier Avenue South. It's a blue storefront with a big blue sign that says "D.A.D.S." Drop by anytime, or visit us at our website: http://www.aboutdads.org. We're here to serve!

BECOMING DADS

ENDNOTES

Peterson, Eugene, *A Long Obedience in the Same Direction*, 2nd edition, InterVarsity Press, Westmont, IL: 2000, p. 11.

U.S. Census Bureau, "Living Arrangements of Children under 18 Years/1 and Marital Status of Parents by Age, Sex, Race, and Hispanic Origin/2 and Selected Characteristics of the Child for all Children 2010," *Current Population Survey*, Table C3. Internet Release Date November, 2010.

Nord, Christine Winquist, and Jerry West. *Fathers' and Mothers' Involvement in their Children's Schools by Family Type and Resident Status*. Table 1. (NCES 2001-032). Washington, DC: U.S. Dept. of Education, National Center of Education Statistics, 2001.

U.S. Census Bureau, "Family Structure and Children's Living Arrangements 2012," *Current Population Report*, July 1, 2012.

McDonald, Shawn, *Rise*, Shawn McDonald, N.d. CD.

Centers for Disease Control and Prevention, "Births: Final Data for 2013," table B. http://www.cdc.gov/nchs/fastats/unmarried-childbearing.htm. Accessed 7 April 2015.

U.S. Census Bureau, *Family Structure and Children's Living Arrangements 2012*. Current Population Report, July 1, 2012. http://www.fathers.com/statistics-and-research/the-extent-of-fatherlessness/. Accessed 7 April 2015.

Matthew 4:1-11

John 10: 14, 27

Jerome G. Miller, "Search and Destroy: The Plight of African American Males in the Criminal Justice System," Alexandria, VA: National Center on Institutions and Alternatives, 1992.

Source: Census Bureau. "Living Arrangements of Children Under 18 Years Old: 1960 to Present." U.S. Census Bureau, July 1, 2012. http://www.census.gov/population/socdemo/hh-fam/ch5.xls.

U.S. Census Bureau, "Children's Living Arrangements and Characteristics:

March 2011," Table C8. Washington D.C.: 2011.

U.S. Department of Health and Human Services, "ASEP Issue Brief: Information on Poverty and Income Statistics," September 12, 2012.

Hoffmann, John P., "The Community Context of Family Structure and Adolescent Drug Use," *Journal of Marriage and Family* 64 (May 2002): 314-330.

U.S. Department of Health and Human Services, National Center for Health Statistics, "Survey on Child Health," Washington, DC, 1993.

Hofferth, S. L. (2006). Residential Father Family Type and Child Well-Being: Investment versus Selection. Demography, 43, 53-78.

The Lancet, Jan. 25, 2003 ▪ Gunilla Ringbäck Weitoft, MD, Centre for Epidemiology, the National Board of Health and Welfare, Stockholm, Sweden ▪ Irwin Sandler, PhD, Professor of Psychology and Director of the Prevention Research Center, Arizona State University, Tempe ▪ Douglas G. Jacobs, MD, Associate Clinical Professor of Psychiatry, Harvard Medical School; and Founder and Director, The National Depression Screening Program ▪ Madelyn Gould, PhD, MPH, Professor of Child Psychiatry and Public Health, College of Physicians and Surgeons, Columbia University; and Research Scientist, New York State Psychiatric Institute. http://www.webmd.com/baby/news/20030123/absent-parent-doubles-child-suicide-risk. Accessed 7 April 2015.

Tillman, K. H. (2007). "Family Structure Pathways and Academic Disadvantage among Adolescents in Stepfamilies," *Journal of Marriage and Family*.

Edward Kruk, Ph.D., "The Vital Importance of Paternal Presence in Children's Lives." May 23, 2012. http://www.psychologytoday.com/blog/co-parenting-after-divorce/201205/father-absence-father-deficit-father-hunger. Accessed 7 April 2015.

Stephen Demuth and Susan L. Brown, "Family Structure, Family Processes, and Adolescent Delinquency: The Significance of Parental Absence Versus Parental Gender," *Journal of Research in Crime and Delinquency* 41, No. 1 (February 2004): 58-81, http://familyfacts.org/briefs/26/marriage-and-family-as-deterrents-from-delinquency-violence-and-crime.
Knoester, C., & Hayne, D.A.,"Community Context, Social Integration into Fam-

ily and Youth Violence," *Journal of Marriage and Family* 67 (2005), 767-780.

Heather A. Turner, "The Effect of Lifetime Victimization on the Mental Health of Children and Adolescents," *Social Science & Medicine*, Vol. 62, No. 1, (January 2006), pp. 13-27.

Hendricks, C.S., Cesario, S.K., Murdaugh, C., Gibbons, M.E., Servonsky, E.J., Bobadilla, R.V., Hendricks, D.L., Spencer-Morgan, B., & Tavakoli, A. (2005).

Teachman, Jay D. "The Childhood Living Arrangements of Children and the Characteristics of Their Marriages," *Journal of Family Issues* 25 (January 2004), 86-111.

Source: U.S. Census Bureau, Current Population Survey, "Living Arrangements of Children under 18 Years/1 and Marital Status of Parents by Age, Sex, Race, and Hispanic Origin/2 and Selected Characteristics of the Child for all Children 2010." Table C3. Accessed 15 July, 2015.

Source: Center for Disease Control and Prevention, National Vital Statistics System, "National Marriage and Divorce Rate Trends." http://www.cdc.gov/nchs/nvss/marriage_divorce_tables.htm Accessed July 15, 2015

Source: U.S. Census Bureau, "Children's Living Arrangements and Characteristics": March 2011, Table C8. Washington, D.C., 2011. Accessed 15 July, 2015.

David Autour and Melanie Wasserman, "Wayward Sons: The Emerging Gender Gap in Education and Labor Markets," Third Way Think Tank: 2015, http://content.thirdway.org/publications/662/Third_Way_Report_-_NEXT_Wayward_Sons-The_Emerging_Gender_Gap_in_Labor_Markets_and_Education.pdf. Accessed 21 July, 2015.

Pew Research Center, Social and Demographic Trends, "The Rise of Single Fathers," http://www.pewsocialtrends.org/2013/07/02/the-rise-of-single-fathers. Accessed 15 July, 2015.

Congressional Research Service, "Spending for Federal Benefits and Services for People With Low Income," http://www.scribd.com/doc/110366590/Spending-for-Federal-Benefits-and-Services-for-People-With-Low-Income-FY08-FY11. Accessed 15 July, 2015.

Gretchen Livingston and Kim Parker, "A Tale of Two Fathers," Social and

Demographic Trends, Pew Research Center: June 15, 2011. http://www.
pewsocialtrends.org/2011/06/15/a-tale-of-two-fathers/#living-apart-from-the-
kids. Accessed 27 September, 2015.

Matthew 3:17

National Fatherhood Initiative, "The Cost of Fatherhood Absence," *Father
Facts*, http://www.fatherhood.org/ff7-sample. Accessed 7 April 2015.